How to LOVE Sales

A Framework to Build Confidence and Success

Paul Kesig

Published by Kesig Enterprise Solutions

Every effort has been made to obtain permissions for materials quoted throughout the book. If any required acknowledgements have been omitted, or any rights overlooked, it is unintentional. Please notify the publisher of any omission, and it will be rectified in future editions.

For permission requests, write to the author at: info@paulkesig.com

Paul Kesig
How to LOVE Sales / Paul Kesig. —1st ed.

Paperback ISBN: 979-8-9904181-0-3
Hardcover ISBN: 979-8-9904181-1-0
Ebook ISBN: 979-8-9904181-2-7

Cover design by Lucy Giller (www.lucygiller.com)
Interior design and formatting by Lucy Giller (www.lucygiller.com)
Editing by Jess Lomas (https://reedsy.com/lomas-jess)

To mom and dad, thanks for recommending sales—I *love* it!

Contents

9 The Journey Ahead   235

References   247

Author's Note

Starting something new is always hard.

One of my passions in life has been sales. From when I was a young kid with a paper route to selling at a retail store during the holidays to having my first territory with over $1,000,000 in revenue, I loved the connections I made with people and the thrill of the sale.

When I told people I was "in sales," they would always tell me they could never do sales. Then they would say it is too hard. This book is my answer to "sales is too hard." Yes, sales is a challenging profession, but you can love it.

My goal in writing this book is to help new sales consultants, people who hate the thought of sales, or current sales professionals looking to improve their skills and learn to love sales.

I do not believe there is a magic formula for you to be successful at sales. You must be willing to dig deep within yourself to determine if you can put in the hard work. You must desire to learn more about yourself and those around you. You must want something more than you have now, both for yourself and those you serve. As the old adage goes: "If you love what you do, you never have to work a day in your life."

I made many mistakes along my sales journey, and I'm sure I will continue to make more and learn from them. However, my hope is that through this book, you can learn from my framework to be successful in sales. God has been patient and gracious with me throughout my career, and He has taught me patience, faithfulness, and joy.

If you are ready to embrace learning and applying new concepts, challenging your skills daily, and getting in touch with your emotional side, then let's start this trek together! I hope you love every minute of the journey!

Acknowledgments

Tara I Thank you for loving me, encouraging me, and playing with me every day. I love you so much and am so blessed to have you as my wife!

Andrew I Your tenacity for life and your all-in mentality help to keep me young and motivated. I am excited to see your success!

Allison I Your tender care yet direct approach makes me smile, brings me great joy, and reminds me that you can be loving and direct. I'm so proud of you!

Mom I Your love, attention, and time are a true gift to me. Thank you for teaching me the importance of asking questions and always being available for people.

Dad I Your passion for knowledge, always improving the process, and ability to fix anything has taught me that with time, patience, and knowledge, anything is possible.

Kathy I Thank you for being an encouraging mother-in-law, one of my biggest fans, and always willing to listen to my crazy ideas!

My Teammates I I have had the privilege to serve alongside many incredibly talented people who always encouraged and challenged me. I feel an incredible sense of belonging and acceptance with each of you. Thank you for always pushing me to raise the bar!

My Friends | Thank you for being willing to laugh with me, encourage me, and push me. You have helped me embrace challenges and pushed me to achieve more than I ever thought possible.

Jesus | Listed last, but first in my life. I am nothing without You and Your love and grace as my guide. Thank you for being my daily support, comfort, and direction! I love you!

13 If I speak human or angelic tongues but do not have love, I am a noisy gong or a clanging cymbal. 2 If I have the gift of prophecy and understand all mysteries and all knowledge, and if I have all faith so that I can move mountains but do not have love, I am nothing. 3 And if I give away all my possessions, and if I give over my body in order to boast but do not have love, I gain nothing.

4 Love is patient, love is kind. Love does not envy, is not boastful, is not arrogant, 5 is not rude, is not self-seeking, is not irritable, and does not keep a record of wrongs. 6 Love finds no joy in unrighteousness but rejoices in the truth. 7 It bears all things, believes all things, hopes all things, endures all things.

8 Love never ends. But as for prophecies, they will come to an end; as for tongues, they will cease; as for knowledge, it will come to an end. 9 For we know in part, and we prophesy in part, 10 but when the perfect comes, the partial will come to an end. 11 When I was a child, I spoke like a child, I thought like a child, I reasoned like a child. When I became a man, I put aside childish things. 12 For now we see only a reflection as in a mirror, but then face to face. Now I know in part, but then I will know fully, as I am fully known. 13 Now these three remain: faith, hope, and love—but the greatest of these is love.

1 CORINTHIANS 13:1-13 (CSB)

The LOVE Sales Framework™

"Another peddler stopped in my office today." Those were the words my father used to say when he came home from work. I would always ask, "What did they want?" His response was, "I don't know, I didn't see them because they didn't make an appointment with me."

Whoa! Now, you either think my father is incredibly rude or that he is completely justified since that sales consultant did not have an appointment.

Let's consider the nuggets in that exchange when it comes to sales.

1. No appointment = no sales.
2. No appointment = no value.
3. No appointment = no connection to the customer.
4. Peddler = annoying.
5. Stopping by = interrupting.

From a young age, I was exposed to the annoying side of sales through my dad. I learned all the things *not* to do in sales from the stories he told at the dinner table.

I was also exposed to the joy of sales through my paper route with customers who tipped. I discovered how to delight my customers when I came by to collect their payment. Hint: bringing chocolate through the various seasons always seemed to help.

In each of these examples, the thing that was consistent was *love*. My dad loved his job, but he hated to be interrupted by someone who did not respect his time. I loved my customers, and I fell in *love* with the feeling of creating a sale and bringing value to people.

This feeling is one of the reasons I chose sales as a profession. I enjoyed seeing the joy that I brought customers through my interactions.

My grandfather, Pap-Pap, died when I was 10 years old and in the fourth grade. I remember going to the hospital in what was a sad time, but I loved the atmosphere. Yes, it was sterile, and yes, it was sad, but I knew everyone there was trying to help people, as the doctors and nurses were doing for my Pap-Pap.

That interaction set me on a trajectory to help people. I knew I did not want to be a doctor, both because of the class content and the amount of schooling I would have to complete, but I did know I wanted to help people in the medical field. Therefore, I worked hard to secure a career in medical device sales. I knew people would always struggle with medical difficulties or challenges and that with the products or services I sold, I could help them have a better quality of life.

I went to school at Ohio University because of The Ralph and Luci Schey Sales Centre, knowing I would have to take specific classes to learn how to be a sales consultant. I loved those classes and learned various sales models. I studied communications as a minor, recognizing the importance of daily dialogue with people and the need to communicate my ideas effectively. During my time in college, I worked retail on my winter breaks. I had a side job selling advertisements on campus for the local TV station, and I was an intern with a large Fortune 15 company, Cardinal Health, to grow my medical industry network.

Fast forward to today, over my 15 years in sales:

- I have sold in the retail, advertising, pharmaceuticals, medical device, and biologics markets.
- I have called on customers such as small "mom-and-pop" organizations and the # 1 hospital system in the United States.
- I have sold in large cities and in rural country towns with more cows than people.
- I have sold products that cost $300 to over $2,000,000 and consistently hit my quota.
- I have won Sales Consultant of the Year awards, glamor trips, fancy plaques, watches, rings, vacations, given a TEDxJNJ Talk, and more.
- I have failed more times than I want to remember.

Throughout all the ups and downs of my sales experience, no matter the customer size, location, product, or service I was selling, there has been one consistent action that has made me successful—*LOVE*.

While selling with *love* may sound crazy, my hope for you is that by the end of this book, you will grow confident in learning to *love* sales, delight your customers, and achieve your goals.

The Importance of Sales in Business

As I was studying in college, my professors always shared that 90% of new college graduates would end up in some type of sales profession. You may have a degree in political science, finance, or journalism, but your first job is likely going to be a sales job. One of the top sales consultants I have worked with actually has a degree in history.

It's important to realize that every day, you either sell something or you are being sold to, whether you know it or not. Sales is the lifeblood of any organization; it's the engine that powers growth, the reason companies hit (or miss) their objectives and the way great ideas get shared and acted upon. No matter where you are in your journey—from your first sales job to being a new business owner, a seasoned entrepreneur, or an aspiring sales professional—congratulations on starting your official sales journey! Understanding and mastering the art of sales is not just important—it's essential for success.

I can say with confidence that 100% of people sell. How? Consider this: every successful product, every groundbreaking service, and every game-changing idea wouldn't have reached its full potential without sales. Somebody was telling someone else about how great that product or service is, and then word spread about how great it was, and all of a sudden, it went viral!

Sales goes beyond simply persuading someone to buy your product for the sake of hitting a quota or making some additional money. Sales is about building relationships, solving problems, and providing value. It's the bridge that connects your offerings to the people who need them, creating a win-win value transfer for both parties involved.

Most companies have a sales department, and if not, there is usually someone who is "doing sales," such as business development, corporate accounts, the company owner, or someone else. However, even if you are not in a formal business or official sales role, do you still sell? YES!

I often hear people say, "I could never do sales, it's too hard. I could never sell anything." Wrong! Each of us sells ideas, recommendations, or interests to people we interact with every day. Let me prove it.

Here is the scenario: you and your significant other are going out on a date after a long week of work. You've both worked hard, and you have the night free. You now need to decide where to go to dinner. Does the conversation sound something like this?

You: "We are going to eat Italian tonight because I *love* Italian."

Other: "Um, I was thinking Mexican."

You: "We cannot eat Mexican because Italian is better. I know you want noodles and a good sauce."

Other: "No, I want tacos, which is why I said Mexican."

Realistically, it probably goes more like this:

You: "Where are you thinking for dinner tonight? I'm in the mood for Italian."

Other: "You know, I am craving some tacos since we haven't had Mexican in a while."

You: "You're right, we haven't had Mexican in a while. Isn't there a new Mexican fusion restaurant we wanted to try?"

Other: "Oh yeah, I remember talking about that place. Let's check out the menu."

Notice the dialogue that occurs. Each of you is selling the other ideas. The more specific you are about where you want to go to dinner, and the more determined they are about their decision, the harder your potential sale to the other person will be. You may have to go to a buffet if you come to an impásse. However, you are both working toward a win-win outcome for you to enjoy date night together.

Consider just how many times you have sold a friend on the best food joint in town, convinced a group of people to go to a concert, or simply worked with a loved one or friend to help them find the best earrings to pair with that perfect outfit.

In an ever-changing world, the role of sales is an increasingly sophisticated craft aimed at bringing value to your customers, whoever they are.

Overcoming Common Sales Fears

If you're new to the world of sales, you might be wondering, "Is sales for me?" Maybe the salespeople you have dealt with have been sly, conniving, self-centered, or dishonest. I'm here to tell you it doesn't have to be this way.

It is normal to be nervous or apprehensive about certain aspects of sales.

- You may not want to look foolish in front of a client by not having an answer.
- You may be afraid of the rejection you will receive from a client.
- You may have anxiety that you will miss quota and be seen as a complete failure to yourself, your peers, or your company.
- You may be uncertain that you even have the skills it takes to succeed in sales. (Hint: you do!)
- You may even feel that the effort or potential rejection just isn't worth it.

When you put all these thoughts together, sales can feel overwhelming before you have even begun.

Consider me your sales coach.

I challenge you to embrace these fears and not let them hold you back from realizing your full potential as a sales professional.

There is good news here. Remember, everyone starts somewhere. The best salespeople weren't born with an innate ability to close deals effortlessly. They developed their skills through learning, practice, and a mindset that embraced growth. They have mastered the art of having grit, being resilient, and perfecting their craft.

My sales journey took me through a range of emotions. I had days where I pounded my steering wheel in frustration. I had days where I ran around my house jumping for joy. I have been laughed at, praised, sworn at, and celebrated. Through all of this, I have learned to *love* sales. My goal is for you to leverage the LOVE Sales Framework™ so that you, too, can *love* sales.

The LOVE Sales Framework™

For me to help you *love* sales, you need something to remember and use as leverage when you are stuck to help you get back on track.

The LOVE Sales Framework™ is the foundation for how to begin to *love* sales. Each letter in LOVE represents a key component in sales and contributes to selling with *love*. Following this framework will help you win sales, increase your confidence, and challenge you to approach each of your customers differently. Let's explore each of the core principles of the LOVE Sale Framework™.

 = **Little Wins:** I'll teach you how to celebrate the small wins that will build your confidence, provide attainable goals, and lead to greater success.

 = **Open-Ended Questions:** Questions are the most important aspect of sales, and to truly *love* sales, you must *love* asking questions. I'll teach you how and why to ask open-ended questions to engage your customers and the best way to listen to their answers that will set you apart from your competition.

 = **Value:** If you know you are providing value to your customer, you will *love* the outcome for both of you. I'll teach you how to identify and communicate the value you bring, how to demonstrate the value of your product or service, and how to overcome objections.

 = **Emotional Connection:** We are all emotional beings and make both emotional and logical decisions. I'll teach you how to build trust and rapport with customers, how to leverage emotional intelligence and build a genuine emotional connection with your customers.

The LOVE Sales Framework™ isn't just a fancy acronym; it's rooted in the *love* you have for others and a genuine desire to help and serve them. It will help you with the concepts needed to be a successful sales consultant. But you must have *love* at the core of your actions to build lasting and meaningful customer connections.

I'm excited to embark on this adventure with you as your sales coach and transform your fears or uncertainties into selling confidently. When we're finished, I hope you love sales as much as I do and that you are ready to take your selling skills to the next level.

2

L = Little Wins

I would drive 1,000 miles per week. That was my metric. If I was driving 1,000 miles per week, I knew I was doing the right amount of activity to make sure I was gathering sales to hit quota. The 1,000 miles was not a company-required number each week, but it did provide me with a good metric for activity that I could quantify. Sometimes, I made more local sales calls, and it would be impossible to do 1,000 miles in a week. Other times, I did more than 1,000 miles in a week if I had to make long drives to customers farther away.

Having this number helped me *love* sales. It gave me a number that I could hold myself accountable to based on the activity that I knew was necessary for success. See, one of my goals was to win 'Sales Consultant of the Year.' This award is given to the top sales consultant each year at the Company's awards ceremony. Each company calculates how you can earn it differently, but the premise is the same—the winner is the best sales consultant in the company that year.

Having a clear goal to strive for—becoming Sales Consultant of the Year— and a strong purpose behind it—helping people—made my motivation to *love* sales palpable.

The L in the LOVE Sales Framework™ stands for Little Wins. Most salespeople are motivated by achieving a goal so that they can make money. I have met a lot of salespeople who tell me that they just want to make a lot of money, and that is why they are in sales.

Yes, you can make a lot of money in sales. No, money should not be your only motivation. If you only focus on the money *you* will earn, you will lose sight of the achievements that you make along the way and the impact you can have on your *customers*. You can build financial goals into what you want to attain, but I would challenge you that monetary reward should not be your only goal, or you will struggle to *love* sales.

How to Define Little Wins in Sales

Living in Northern New England for over 10 years, I was able to hike some incredible mountains in New Hampshire, Maine, and Vermont. One of my favorite hikes was Mount Moosilauke in New Hampshire. A friend and I got up early on a Saturday morning and drove to base camp. We had all our day gear packed with snacks, lunch, water, and layers for the hike. We had the proper shoes and, of course, a camera to take pictures along the way.

As with any hike, the start of the climb is usually quite fun. On this particular climb, we were deep in the woods, so it was dark and filled with trees. The ground was covered in a blanket of red leaves since the foliage was in peak season. We had lots of energy as we started the gradual hike from the trailhead. As we continued and got about 30 minutes into our hike, the terrain became rockier and steeper! We had to walk single file and worked together to point out places to step so that we didn't twist an ankle along the way.

Finally, over an hour into the hike, we caught our first glimpse of the valley below. It was a small viewing spot off the trail, and we stopped for a snack and some water. We were even more excited to get to the summit with the tease that we saw on that side trail. The further we went up the mountain, the more our legs burned, our breath became shorter, the air felt different, and then, eventually, the tree line faded away.

I always thought it was so cool to climb above the tree line and start to scale the granite slabs in the White Mountains. As we came out of the tree line, we could see the summit and pushed with all our might to get there, knowing the reward of the view and the lunch we packed when we arrived.

The view did not disappoint, and we took pictures, high-fived, and ate our lunch. We had made it to the summit. However, we now had to make it back down the mountain to get to our car before nightfall. We decided to take a different trail down so that we could have different views.

After about ten to fifteen minutes into our hike down, we got caught up in the clouds. These fast, sweeping, white-mist clouds were whipping over the granite rocks as we descended from the summit. My friend was no more than 10 feet in front of me, yet I could not see him through the whiteout. The temperature plummeted, and it was hard to see the trail markers. Just a few minutes before, we were taking in the incredible views at the top, and now we could barely make out the cairn trail markers guiding our way.

Walking through the mist was both nerve-wracking and exhilarating! Both of us loved the smell of the clouds, the feel of the mist, and the power of the wind as we descended. We had never been "in a cloud" before (even though people at times have told me my head was in the clouds). Eventually, after 20 more minutes, we started to descend into the tree line, and the mist faded away.

The descent was not as physically demanding as the hike up the mountain, but it still required skill to avoid stepping in a hole or losing our balance and falling. The climb down is more methodical to find your footing versus the climb up. We both made it down safely and as we were getting into our car we saw a moose standing 15 yards off into the woods by the trailhead. We both thought it was apropos to see a moose at Mt. Moosilauke.

Sales is a lot like climbing a mountain while climbing another mountain simultaneously. And another. And another.

As you go through the sales process, you are climbing various mountains with each of your customers. They're not all on the same mountain; each one is going to look different and have different terrain, obstacles, and views. You are going to have summit moments and side trail views. You are also going to have mist, moose, and poor footholds on your journey.

You must realize that to be successful in sales, part of the way to *love* sales is to know that your journey with a customer never stops. Even when they say yes and buy your product or service, the top sales consultants will continue to service those customers and build the relationship. You don't reach the summit of the mountain and then call a helicopter to come pick you up and take you down.

This is why little wins are so important. The views and experiences along the journey are what help keep you motivated to achieve your goal. Seeing the scenery, the side trails, the tree line, the granite, the mist, and the summit are all little wins along the way. Getting through a particularly difficult part of the trail is a win. Making it up and down the mountain is a win.

Focusing on the small, incremental victories over time will collectively contribute to your overall success.

In sales, little wins can take on various forms, including:

- making a successful cold call
- asking a great question that kept the conversation going
- completing one more call/visit that gave you additional knowledge
- meeting a new stakeholder in the account
- nurturing a lead from initial interest to a deeper engagement
- getting a prospect to agree to a follow-up meeting
- handling an objection effectively
- anticipating an objection and being ready to handle it
- getting an order for one item
- getting an order for two items (or more)
- getting one order in a week
- getting two orders in a week (or more)

- securing a smaller sale at a new account that can lead to a larger one in the future
- getting an order at a new account for the first time
- having a conversation about an industry concept and building a customer connection
- attending your first trade show
- signing up your first prospect
- delivering your first proposal
- refining your proposal presentation.

Obviously, this is not an exhaustive list. You know your business and personal skill level best and have the greatest opportunity to set realistic goals to achieve. For me, it was focusing on the frequency of calls, orders, activities, and conversations so that I could get one order in a day/week/month, depending on the customer I was working on.

Be mindful that if your goal is too big, you'll be de-motivated, and that will make you *hate* sales! Just like hiking a mountain, my friend and I hiked based on our experience level. We didn't do an easy hike, but we didn't pick the hardest peak to scale in the White Mountains either. The hardest peak may be a longer-term goal, but our Mt. Moosilauke hike was a little win along our journey of hiking the various peaks in Northern New England.

Setting Realistic Goals and Expectations

I want to bench 500 pounds. That is completely unrealistic for me. I'm not a bodybuilder. I know there are people who can lift that amount, but I also know my personal limits, and 500 pounds is not in my future (or past).

I want to run a Spartan race. Now, that is an ambitious goal for me, but I think I can make it happen (more on that later).

Set goals you want to achieve. Dream big! Be ambitious! My goal to win Sales Consultant of the Year was ambitious. It is only given to one person per company per year. To achieve that goal, I knew I would have to do things other people were not willing to do. I would have to sacrifice certain activities (e.g., watching TV) to plan out my prospects, accounts, strategy, and call schedule so that I could maximize my chances of winning.

The best part was that the rest of the sales consultants in my company were also trying to be Sales Consultant of the Year, so it was a very competitive task. To achieve something great, you need to break it down into achievable actions—little wins.

These little wins should be realistic in helping you achieve your ambitious goals. You should know yourself well enough that you will be willing and able to follow through on the goals that you set. Some people will say getting up at 4:00 AM each day will make you successful. Driving 1,000 miles a week may get you to your goal. However, neither of these may be realistic for you and your circumstances.

To effectively focus on setting realistic goals, you should understand the following areas at a minimum.

KNOW YOUR NUMBERS

Begin by analyzing your sales data and understanding your current sales territory performance:

- How many calls or meetings do you need to close a sale?
- What's your conversion rate from leads to customers?
- What's your target revenue to hit your objective?
- What does your leadership team expect out of your territory?
- What's the condition of your territory (strong market share, poor penetration, highly competitive, saturated, large, small?)

If you don't know how much you need to sell in a particular timeframe, how are you going to measure if the activities you are doing are going to be successful? Even more, how are you going to set up little wins along the way to help you achieve your goal?

Each territory is unique, so begin by analyzing your numbers so that you can best set yourself up for success.

BREAK DOWN YOUR GOALS

Instead of setting vague goals like "increase sales," break them down into smaller, more manageable targets. Let's say your goal is to get six new customers a year. You can review your numbers to identify accounts where you can grow business, or you can set a goal to have a new customer every two months so that you hit your goal. You can also define the right amount of activity that is needed for those conversions so that you prepare appropriately to hit your goal.

I was coaching a sales consultant who wanted to win a luxury trip with her company that year. She had just started in a new territory and was having trouble realizing how she was going to hit her goal. I challenged her to break down her overall number into a daily sales number. We did the math together by taking her overall quota and dividing it by the number of working days in the year. This helped her have a specific number to go after. We then were able to break it down into monthly and quarterly targets so that she could measure if she was on track. At the end of our conversation, she smiled and realized that she only needed to convert four customers that year to be able to hit her goals, which guided her efforts to prospect more effectively.

As my father told me growing up: "If you don't know where you're going, all roads lead there."

The same is true if you don't break down your goals. If you don't know what you need to sell today, this month, or this quarter, how will you know if you are on track to achieve your goal of hitting quota or reaching your more ambitious goals?

There is more detail in Chapter 8 on how to break down your goals to find business and build metrics.

PRIORITIZE YOUR EFFORTS

If you were going to run a marathon, would you only do pull-ups? Of course not! You would focus on building your leg strength and breathing endurance by spending time outside jogging or on the treadmill.

The same is true of sales! You need to prioritize and focus on the activities that will have the most significant impact on your territory. For instance, if you drive two hours to visit a target that can only contribute 10% to your overall objective, how are you going to hit the other 90%? However, if you had an account that could potentially contribute 60% of your business and was two and a half hours away, which one would you choose?

Yes, me too. I would drive the longer distance to get more sales. When I was selling point-of-care devices to hospitals, I had an account that was seven and a half hours from my house door-to-door. The drive was a doozy, but if I converted that account, it would be my quota for the year. Over the course of eight months, I did that seven-and-a-half-hour one-way drive two to three times per month. This long drive also gave me plenty of opportunities to look for new business on my drive back home.

I realized I could drive an hour away to a very large customer, but my potential conversion opportunity was very small, whereas my seven-and-a-half-hour drive had an extremely high conversion opportunity. Given the size of the opportunity, what it would mean for my own territory numbers, and the likelihood of closing the deal, I embraced that drive.

Side note: a seven-and-a-half-hour drive gives you a tremendous opportunity to invest in yourself and learn new skills. You can listen to sales books, podcasts, biographies, or any other types of skill development programs to invest in yourself while you are completing the necessary sales activities. This is a little win-win as you are growing your sales and your skills.

Prioritizing effort isn't limited to prospective customers; it can also apply to current ones. If you already have some business with an account, identify a little win that you can set for yourself for growth in that account and prioritize it appropriately. It is much easier to build business in an account where you already have sales and access than it is to start completely from scratch.

Think also of your personality. You are unique, and you connect with people in a unique way. Find stakeholders at accounts where you may connect better than your competition. Leverage your own best traits and set goals accordingly.

If you prioritize where you spend your time to maximize your potential close rate, you will *love* sales!

TIME-BOUND GOAL

I wanted to have my first sale within three months of my start date. Given my product, onboarding, and territory, that was my goal. For me and my industry and product, it was realistic. It was also important for me to set this deadline so I could hold myself accountable for achieving it. Without a deadline, I did not have as much urgency.

Leveraging SMART goals is a great way to create goals that can be achieved (Mind Tools Content Team 2023). In a later chapter, I'll show you more of the SMART goal model, but for now, know that SMART is an acronym for:

S = Specific

M = Measurable

A = Achievable

R = Relevant

T = Timebound

Let me share one of my SMART goals. In early 2023, my family joined a gym so that we could prioritize our health and stay fit. As I was training at the gym, my wife informed me of a Spartan Race and that some gym members were preparing to run it.

A Spartan Race covers various distances (5K, 10K, 25K, etc.) with a number of obstacles around the course (20–30 depending on length). The obstacles could include monkey bars, rope climbs, atlas carry, spear throw, cargo net climb, and others. Training for this race required a full-body workout since it involved running, lifting, throwing, and more. Each finisher of a Spartan race earns a medal and bragging rights for finishing.

GOAL: To successfully complete the 5K Sprint Spartan Race in August of 2023.

Is my goal SMART?

- **Specific**
  - ☐ *Evaluation:* I know the race I am completing and when: Spartan Race in August of 2023.
  - ☐ Verdict: Specific ☑

- **Measurable**
  - ☐ *Evaluation:* I know what I need to do. Complete a Spartan Race. I can measure this by taking a picture of me holding the medal at the end of the race.
  - ☐ Verdict: Measurable ☑

- **Achievable**
  - ☐ *Evaluation:* With proper training, and since it was summer, I had enough time that I could achieve training for the obstacles and running a 5K.
  - ☐ Verdict: Achievable ☑

- **Relevant**
  - ☐ *Evaluation:* This goal fits into my fitness journey goals and would contribute to my overall health.
  - ☐ Verdict: Relevant ☑

- **Time-bound**
  - ☐ *Evaluation:* A specific date was set, August 2023, to complete *the race.*
  - ☐ Verdict: Time-bound ☑

I'm proud to say that I did complete the race, and it far surpassed my expectations. Since my original race, I have run other Spartan races, and my family has joined me, too.

ADJUST AS NECESSARY

While your quota may not change, your goals should be flexible to make sure you are on track to achieving your sales objective.

If you notice that certain activities are consistently stopping you from achieving little wins, adjust your goals and strategies accordingly.

When I was two and a half years into a sales territory, I realized that my way of taking notes was not as effective as it could be. I was using a pad of paper in a folio for each individual customer. I was then required to use a file system in my trunk with each customer and would keep the master files in my house. During my call planning, I would bring my master files from my house and put them in my trunk file system so I would have the information for each customer. As I spent time organizing and continually moving these files around, I wondered if there was a way I could leverage technology to be more efficient.

Around this same time, the original iPad came out. I had invested in a new iPad to keep my notes all in one spot. The problem was I did not have a good system to follow. I wanted to write my notes down like I always did with a pen and paper because it was quicker during customer meetings. I couldn't type during a sales call, so I was struggling to find a way to make my system work the way that I wanted it to, even with all my research.

One day, I called on a senior leader in an account for the first time, and when he walked in, he took out his iPad, a capacitive stylus, and created the meeting in an app on his iPad. In that moment, I completely changed my entire approach to the meeting and started asking him questions about technology! What app was he using? What stylus was he using? How effective was the program? Since this customer also loved technology and was just starting to use this app, he was kind enough to answer my questions. We eventually talked business in that call, but we connected over technology first.

After that meeting, I completely overhauled my notetaking experience. I downloaded the app he recommended on my iPad, and I started to practice taking notes. I was also able to consolidate all my paper records into that one iPad app, which made me much more productive during my time in the field and when I got home. When my manager would ride with me, I was able to quickly check on each account and give a status update because I had all my files at my fingertips.

Keep in mind, by this point, I had been in sales for several years, so my current approach was working. However, I realized there was room for improvement. Lots of my peers were still using pen and paper to take notes, and some still do to this day. I wanted to remain competitive in my territory. I knew I was competing with myself to be the most productive, competitive, and efficient consultant so that I could achieve my goals.

You will develop your own process in sales, and it will work, but I challenge you to continually assess your process so that you can become the best. Don't just do an overhaul of your systems because a certain time has passed or a new technology has arrived. Think deeply about what you will gain and how it will impact your ability to serve your customers. My goal in improving my notetaking was to help me be more efficient in tracking customer information and speed up my follow-up time to provide the highest level of service.

Evaluate your goals and processes, adjust as necessary so that you can achieve them, and you will *love* sales.

Celebrate Small Achievements

Did you get a first meeting with a customer? Congratulations! Treat yourself to a small reward.

Did you close your first sale? Congratulations! Treat yourself to a reward.

Did you finally close that big contract that helped you surpass your quota? Congratulations! Definitely celebrate!

I like to compare celebrating small achievements to the joy of parents with their newborn baby. Watching new parents is always so much fun. Every time their baby does something for the first time, they are ecstatic, and they tell everyone about it! Did the baby smile? Celebrate! Did the baby coo? Celebrate! Did the baby say "Dada" or "Mama"? Cue the big celebration! It keeps going with sitting up, crawling, first steps, first words, and more. You will naturally celebrate these moments when you are a parent, so why would you not celebrate your small achievements when you are in sales?

Don't be too rigid to realize that sales is a process, and you will probably not have sales "parents" to cheer you on each step of the way. You are going to need to self-celebrate those little wins to keep you motivated and to be ready to tackle the obstacles. Just as you probably loved hearing your parents' praise when you did something right as a kid, celebrating those little wins as you get into sales can have a big impact on your motivation and self-confidence. How? Let's find out.

CELEBRATING LITTLE WINS BOOSTS YOUR CONFIDENCE

When you celebrate your successes, no matter how small they may seem, you reinforce the belief that you are capable of achieving your goals. This confidence, in turn, makes you more effective in your sales efforts.

I'll talk more about building your confidence and resilience in a later chapter. In short, think of confidence as how you view yourself and your abilities, not how someone else views you. If you believe you are competent, capable, and committed, you will show up confident even if you don't feel like it.

When learning to walk as a child, you fall down a lot! Those first steps are shaky and uncertain, and only a couple happen at a time. But on the other end, your parents were probably holding out their arms, smiling big, and cheering you on the entire time!

In sales, your first few calls (steps) will be shaky and uncertain but know you have what it takes to be successful. Keep practicing. When you fall down, keep getting up and work to get better every single day. Then, make sure to celebrate your achievements on a regular basis.

CELEBRATING LITTLE WINS MOTIVATES YOUR PROGRESS

Once you are celebrating your little win achievements, you will continue to stay motivated. After you take those first few steps as a child, you learn the freedom you get by being able to move. That baby now wants to go and explore EVERYTHING! They may not be able to move too fast yet, but they are highly motivated to explore their surroundings.

As you celebrate your little wins, it will help you intentionally focus on what you accomplished, and this will help motivate you to get even more little wins. As the saying goes: "success begets success," which means that the more success you have, the more likely you are to continue to be successful.

When you achieve your little win, who will you tell?

When a baby takes their first steps, who do the parents tell? Correct, everyone! I used to celebrate my little wins with my family. We would either go out for a treat like ice cream or a cookie, or, depending on how big the win was, I would take them out for a special meal. Involving others in my celebration of success helped hold me accountable for the results but also allowed me to share the experience, making the goal more achievable.

CELEBRATING LITTLE WINS CREATES A POSITIVE ENVIRONMENT

Having others involved in celebrating the little wins helps create a positive environment both at work and at home. Other sales consultants you are competing with are probably not going to be ecstatic to hear about your sales success, but loved ones, friends, or coaches will absolutely want to celebrate with you.

If you work on a sales team or pod larger than just you individually, make sure to include everyone in the celebration of the little win. This inclusion will encourage teamwork and camaraderie and build a culture of achievement.

My most effective sales managers always sent out notes to the entire team when other consultants had successful wins. The more frequently this communication occurred, the more camaraderie the team had and the more positive the conversations among team members were.

For you to *love* sales, you will have to celebrate your little wins. Whenever I converted a large customer, after many small wins, I would get a t-shirt from the local area to remind me of my accomplishment. Then, each time I wore the t-shirt, it would remind me of my victory and the hard work it took to achieve it. Little wins will help boost your confidence, keep you motivated about the progress you are making, and create a positive environment for yourself and your team to operate in. You can do it! Now go celebrate getting it done!

Building Confidence through Small Successes

In the book *The Leadership Secrets of Nick Saban*, Nick Talty talks about how Nick Saban teaches his University of Alabama football players to win each down (Talty, 2022). Saban emphasizes the importance of focusing on winning first down, then second down, then third down, and finally fourth down. By staying present in each moment and concentrating on the task at hand, Saban believes his players will not only achieve short-term success but also work towards their long-term goals, all while ignoring critics and distractions.

Furthermore, Saban's strategy remains consistent regardless of the score. Whether his team is up by 20-plus points or down by 20-plus points, the emphasis on winning each down provides the stability needed to maximize their chances of winning the game and achieving their goal (Talty, 2022).

Each sales call is an opportunity to build your confidence.

If you focus on little wins, you are going to start to see the achievement of your goals. If you are confident in your skills and the product or service you are selling, you can be successful in sales. Therefore, little wins become part of the foundation for achieving your goals and building your confidence.

EVIDENCE OF PROGRESS

Let me ask you something. Do you look exactly the way you want to look after you work out for the first time? It's doubtful. Exercise is a long game to see results. You must be consistent with going to the gym on a regular basis to achieve the results you want and to hit your goals.

In sales, your first call is going to sound funny and feel unnatural. You are going to think you need to talk a lot and show the customer your product immediately (because they obviously want to buy it right now!). You are going to stumble over the questions you ask, the features and benefits you are memorizing from your training, and getting the next steps.

Guess what? Your second, third, and fourth calls are also going to feel unnatural. I cannot tell you exactly when it will feel natural. Just like working out, the more you lift and practice, the more fluid and stronger you will become.

Keep practicing daily.

If you are diligent in practicing how you research the customer, start the meeting with them, the questions you ask, when you bring up your products, and how you close for the next actionable item, you will start to see success. Each little win is tangible evidence that you are making progress and a nice reminder that you are on the right track. It will take time to get to the heavier weights, but you will get there.

LEARNING OPPORTUNITIES

Little wins often come with valuable lessons. Whether it's a successful sales call or a closed deal, there is something to learn from every achievement. As you continue to learn, you will continue to enhance your skills and expertise.

I had a large, competitive health system in my territory that accounted for over 35% of the territory's revenue. If I won an account of this size, it would mean success for multiple years. As I was getting acclimated to my territory, I had to meet with a senior leader at the account who was considered an expert in the industry. He was a known speaker and sought after for his knowledge in his field of expertise. He had many more years of tenure and experience in the industry than me and had a reputation as being "tough" with reps.

Now, do you think I showed up and told him a thing or two?! Absolutely not. I wanted to learn a thing or two from him! I started by asking questions to understand him as a person and a buyer. I did not expect to close him on my first sale, but I did want to learn from each of our interactions.

Over the course of two years, I called on him faithfully and discussed the value that my products could provide to his healthcare system. After over two years of valuable calls and discussions, he signed a $2,000,000 contract for me that helped me achieve my goals. I had learned what was important to him. I had built my confidence as I continued to practice my skills with other accounts and overcome objections. I took each interaction as a way for me to better learn my craft of sales.

As he was signing the contract, he said that I reminded him of the Dr. Seuss book *Green Eggs and Ham*. In that book, Sam-I-am continues to ask the main character if he wants to try green eggs and ham. His answer is repeatedly no, and then one day, the main character says yes to try them, and it turns out he really likes green eggs and ham.

How did I accomplish this large sale?

1. I did not pester this expert each time we met together.
2. I had set little goals for me to learn more about him and how I could bring him value.
3. I set goals for how often I wanted to connect with him so that I could learn if it was realistic or not.
4. I read industry articles to increase my knowledge so we could have more stimulating conversations.
5. I researched and learned so that I could bring him something new or relevant to the industry.
6. I respected his time, his knowledge, and his system.
7. I continually learned through my little wins of ways that I could make an impact on him and his practice.

To *love* sales, you must continually learn about yourself, your products, your industry, and your customers while setting your goals and celebrating little wins to achieve them.

SUCCESS BREEDS MORE SUCCESS

When my industry expert signed the contract mentioned above, it didn't come with a guarantee for business. Instead, the contract enabled all facilities to purchase my product at a discounted rate. It became my responsibility to convert business across the entire health system.

With that signed contract, I set new little wins. I could now track which decision-makers I still needed to meet and which accounts were ordering (or not). As a result of that signed contract, I was able to grow the overall account with satellite locations to over $2,000,000 and had success where doors and access were once unavailable. It also helped me to get access to new customers in my territory because of the name recognition of those who were now using my products.

This is true for little wins as well. The more you practice and reward the development of your skills, the better you will become at them. The first time you ask a question, it will feel weird. The hundredth time you awsk a question, it will feel better. The thousandth will be even better, and so on. Pick a skill you want to work on and commit to practicing it and figuring out your little wins around it.

Some examples of skills to practice to *love* sales include:

- communication
- presenting
- asking questions
- curiosity
- negotiation
- patience
- time management
- and more.

Little wins are the first part of the LOVE Sales Framework™ and will help you set realistic goals and expectations. Celebrating your little wins will help you see what you have accomplished and improve your confidence as you progress through your sales journey. Remember to embrace each small success, learn from it, and let it propel you closer to achieving your sales goals. You must embrace being sore today so that you can become strong tomorrow.

Questions to Consider

Asking questions is a great place to start for skill development. Start with:

1. What little win can I achieve today? Tomorrow? Next week? Next month?

2. What's stopping me from setting a small goal? What am I afraid of?

3. What SMART Goal can I identify right now to help me grow?

4. What skills or actions do I need to continue to practice to achieve the outcome I want to boost my confidence?

5. When I achieve my little wins, how am I going to celebrate? What is realistic?

6. What adjustments do I need to make to my process or thinking?

7. How am I going to hold myself accountable for these small wins?

8. Who can I include in my celebrations?

3

O = Open-Ended Questions

How are you feeling?

Where do you want to eat tonight?

What's your favorite hobby?

What did you do this weekend?

What's your process for bringing in new products/services?

How would having a dedicated support person on-site impact your inventory management?

What impact would it have if you could finish your case 10–15 minutes earlier by using this product?

In sales, asking questions is the key to uncovering information. As Jeffrey Gitomer says in *The Little Red Book of Selling*, "Ask smart questions, they think you're smart. Ask dumb..." (Gitomer 2004, 117).

In sales, you are known by the questions you ask. Yes, that is a bold statement, but questions are the primary way you engage and interact with a customer. To be seen as smart, you need to ask smart, thought-provoking questions.

If questions are so powerful, why do so many sales consultants not practice asking or perfecting their questioning skills? Because it's hard! There are many factors that go into asking a good question, but most sales consultants default to a close-ended question that doesn't provide many answers. Tell me if this sounds familiar:

CONSULTANT: Hey Jane, how are you doing today?

CUSTOMER: Fine.

CONSULTANT: Are you happy with what you are currently using?

CUSTOMER: Yes.

CONSULTANT: Okay, is there anything you would change about your current product?

CUSTOMER: No.

CONSULTANT: Okay, when would be a good time for me to stop by again?

CUSTOMER: ...

Yikes! That was awkward! What happens next? Usually, because the customer has stopped talking, you, as the sales consultant, will immediately go into demonstrating the features and benefits of your product. Hmm, I wonder how that is going to go.

If you want a more proven way to engage with customers that will help uncover needs so that you can close more sales and *love* sales, keep reading.

In this chapter, we cover the "O" in the LOVE Sales Framework™, which discusses Open-Ended Questions. Using these types of questions can lead to powerful conversations. We will discuss the difference between open-ended and close-ended questions and how to craft an open-ended question effectively. Finally, while asking questions is good, we will spend time on how to effectively listen to the answers so that you can engage better in follow-up questions.

The Power of Open-Ended Questions

If you want to learn to *love* sales, you need to learn to *love* asking questions. When you think of a sales consultant, you may think of someone who is naturally more curious. Or you may think of someone more obnoxious. Think a little deeper here. Those naturally curious people, what type of questions do they ask? What about the obnoxious type? There is usually a difference.

Remember the example in Chapter 1 about going out to dinner with a friend and what the dialogue would look like? You naturally ask questions about what the other person wants, listen to what they are saying, and then come to a mutually beneficial conclusion. This applies to hobbies, sports teams, vacation locations, and many more scenarios.

When a holiday is coming up, what do you ask? "What are you doing for _____?" Hmm, that sounds open-ended to me.

The same is true for your customers. They will tell you things that you want to know, most of the time, if you ask valuable, open-ended questions to hear what is important to them.

You now have no more excuses! You have the power to ask great open-ended questions, you just need some coaching on how to become great at it. I bet you are more curious than you think. Let's find out.

WHAT ARE OPEN-ENDED QUESTIONS?

I have a challenge for you. Before you read any further, let's do an exercise together. I want you to think of an open-ended question that starts with "Have you." You may start with:

- Have you ever...
- Have you seen...
- Have you heard...
- Have you been...
- Have you had...

Okay, write your question here:

_____

_____

_____

How did you do?! Were you able to come up with an open-ended question starting with "Have you?" No? That's because when you start a question with "Have you," the answer will always be "Yes" or "No." Let's use those prompts and see if we can get an open-ended answer.

- Have you ever gotten stuck on the side of the road? – Yes/No
- Have you seen the new device that was just released? – Yes/No
- Have you heard of XYZ, a customer who is now using this product? – Yes/No
- Have you been able to get the results that you want from this service? – Yes/No
- Have you had issues with customer service or billing? – Yes/No

No matter how many words or vivid pictures you paint after the "Have you" prompt, you will get a yes/no response. Now, I hear your objection. You can ask this question and then just follow it up by asking why. That is true, but why would you want to start by getting the customer to agree or disagree with you? The goal should be to start with creating dialogue, not just getting yes or no answers.

There are other phrases that will only give you a yes or no response when asked, too. These include:

1. Can you...
2. Did you...
3. Will you...
4. Are you...
5. Is this...
6. Will this...
7. Can this...
8. Has this...

There are plenty more phrases, but you can catch my drift here: open-ended questions create dialogue, and the prompt at the beginning of the question is important. Open-ended questions invite people to express their thoughts, feelings, and opinions, creating space for richer, more detailed responses.

Let's do another challenge: How can you change your earlier "Have you" question to be open-ended? As you think about this exercise, think about questions that you would naturally ask to learn more about someone.

Write your new question here:

_____

_____

_____

Congratulations, you just re-framed your perspective on asking questions! Remember, the goal of leveraging open-ended questions is to get the customer talking about what's important to them so that you, as the sales consultant, can determine if the product or service you are selling will bring them value and help them.

Did you catch those two important words? Value and help. Later, we will talk about the V in the LOVE Sales Framework™, which focuses more on value.

To *love* sales, you must take the time to craft thought-provoking questions that elicit more than a one-word response. Here are a few open-ended prompts to get you started on your question-writing journey:

1. What is your process for bringing in _____?
2. How would having a dedicated support person on-site help you _____?
3. What impact would it have for you if you could ___?
4. Who else should I speak to about _____?
5. How are you feeling about _____?

CONTRASTING OPEN-ENDED AND CLOSE-ENDED QUESTIONS

You can see how close-ended questions do not create a dialogue. In contrast, open-ended questions help to open a dialogue and get the customer talking. It helps bridge connections both for you as the sales consultant and for the customer. Let's go back to our earlier example and use some open-ended questions instead.

CONSULTANT: Hey Jane, what did you think of that game this weekend?

CUSTOMER: Oh wow, I couldn't believe how close it was. We should have beat them a whole lot sooner, so it wasn't such a nailbiter!

CONSULTANT: I completely agree! But it sure was a fun game! If you have a minute, I'm curious to understand more about how you are using Product A with your clients?

CUSTOMER: I started using Product A right out of college, and I really like how easy it is to operate. I realize it's not perfect, but I'm really familiar with it.

CONSULTANT: I can understand how familiarity helps you be confident. If I could show you a product that could save you time with your inventory process, what impact would that have on your day?

CUSTOMER: Whoa, that's a big claim. I'm always interested in saving time with my inventory so I can be more efficient.

CONSULTANT: That makes sense. When would you have a few minutes for me to showcase Product B and the time-saving impact it could potentially have for you?

CUSTOMER: If you can really save me time like you say you can, I would love to see Product B. I'll be in my office tomorrow at 8:00 AM. Let's meet then.

CONSULTANT: Perfect, I'll see you then! Thanks for your time today.

Notice the difference in the dialogue. Also, notice we didn't convert the customer during this discussion. The little win was getting a follow-up appointment and asking solid, open-ended questions. Having a dialogue will not naturally result in another meeting (you have to decide what next step you are working towards with your customer), but each meeting will provide additional information that can be used in future interactions. Let's consider some of the benefits of asking open-ended questions.

BENEFITS OF USING OPEN-ENDED QUESTIONS IN SALES

Uncover Needs and Pain Points

Open-ended questions encourage customers to share their challenges and aspirations, helping you better understand their needs. If you don't understand what is bothering, affecting, or concerning the customer, you will never be able to fulfill their need with your product or service. Gartner defines a pain point as "any problems the customer may experience along their journey" (Garter n.d.).

Notice our open-ended questions from earlier. The customer was only using the product because she was familiar with it from prior experience. Without our open-ended questions, we wouldn't have known this information.

Think about when you are involved in a sales situation. How often do you openly share your exact need or pain point with the sales consultant? Better yet, how often do you actually even *know* what your exact need or pain point is at the moment? Sometimes, the need or pain point can be very clear. For instance, if the evening is approaching, you are going to need to eat dinner. However, where you eat dinner can be influenced by the questions you ask yourself or your friends.

Remember, as a sales consultant, you will likely be bringing up a problem or need that the customer doesn't realize they have or doesn't want to talk about. That is part of the challenge of sales—getting customers to think about their pain points and needs and walking them through the change process.

Build Rapport

Rapport, in its most basic form, is connection. How do you connect with people? A better question is, how do you like people to connect with you? Some of you probably like text. Others may prefer something on social media. Still, others may want to connect through email or over the phone. Just like you are unique in the way you enjoy connecting, you must be willing to connect with others in the way in which they want to be connected to build rapport.

Open-ended questions can foster a sense of collaboration, demonstrating that you value the customer's input and perspective.

Open-ended questions help the customer understand that you are curious about them and what they have to say versus what you need to sell to hit your quota.

Think of the last telemarketer call or solicitation you received. Were you excited to get that call and have them tell you what you have been missing out on? Probably not! I'm going to assume that you couldn't wait to delete the message or get off the phone and didn't have any interest in what they were selling (if you were even still listening). Did this person build any type of connection with you? Is this how you approach your customers?

Trying to pitch your product immediately after asking a couple of poor, close-ended questions is not a good way to build a connection. Rapport takes time because building connections takes time. Leverage asking open-ended questions to learn about your customers and build those connections to help you be the valuable resource your customer trusts with their situations.

Establish Trust

Truth can also be framed as the belief in the reliability or strength of something or someone. If someone tells you the truth, they are seen as reliable. I remember growing up, my parents always told me that if you tell the truth, you never have to remember what you said.

To *love* sales, you must tell your customers the truth. If you cannot fulfill an order, tell them the truth. If you cannot get a charge reversed, tell the truth. If your product is on backorder, tell the truth. The truth will come out in some way, so it is better to be honest and truthful with your customers. Not telling the truth can make it look like you are trying to deceive them and make yourself look good.

When I am training new sales consultants, they usually do not know much about the products they are selling yet. However, during selling scenarios, they always try to show that they know more than they do. I'll ask them a question that I know the answer to and see if they are willing to tell me that they don't know and will find out and get back to me.

One of my co-workers shared a story when he was calling on a doctor in the Operating Room (OR). This type of sales is intense, and trust is imperative between a doctor and a sales consultant. During the case, the doctor turned around and asked him about an obscure ligament that the consultant had never heard of before. The sales consultant promptly said that he had studied a lot of anatomy to be prepared for this role, but he had never heard of that particular ligament. He would go home and study more about it to make sure he was best prepared to help the next time he was in that surgeon's OR. The doctor then said the consultant could continue to be in his OR since the doctor had made up the ligament to see if the sales consultant would lie to him and tell him all about something that does not exist just to look good. This interaction built trust and honesty between the two of them, so they were prepared when an even larger problem arose.

Not knowing the answer can actually work to your advantage as a sales consultant.

You have the opportunity to follow up again with the customer and learn more about your product or service to better support your customers in the future. Big caveat here: if you are supposed to know the answer and you do not, it is still important to tell the truth. Do not leverage the "I don't know" response as a way to keep getting in front of your customers. That tactic is just as deceitful as not telling them the truth.

Open-ended questions show that you are genuinely interested in helping your customer, which builds trust and credibility. If you communicate well with open-ended questions, are clear about whether your product or service will be a fit for the customer, and then are responsible to do what you said you'd do, you will build trust with your customers.

Zig Ziglar famously said, "If people like you, they'll listen to you, but if they trust you, they'll do business with you." Think about people you trust and why. Do they do what they say they will? Do they care about you? Do you have confidence that what you tell them will stay confidential?

Most of the time, a sales consultant is portrayed as self-focused, greedy, shady, and manipulative. Hmm, I wonder if this is why people are afraid to be in sales? However, sales consultants who *love* sales work with their customers to identify needs, service their needs, and clearly communicate throughout the process, which develops trust between the sales consultant and the customer. Notice how trust takes time to build in your own personal relationships. Remember, it can take the same or longer amount of time and effort in professional relationships.

Crafting Effective Open-Ended Questions

UNDERSTAND YOUR CUSTOMER'S NEEDS

In all my years of selling, I never had a customer walk up to me and tell me exactly what they needed. In all my years of parenting, my kids have told me what they need all the time! I'm not surprised by either of these. My job as a sales consultant is to uncover what my customer needs, determine if my product or service will meet that need, and deliver more value than the customer expects.

If your customer is not going to tell you what they need, what do you have to do? Ask questions. This is more like a teenager. When I was a teenager, my mother used to ask me, "How was your day?" My answer was, "Fine." Or she asked, "How was your math test?" My answer was, "Fine."

You can see how this conversation was very productive—not! To her credit, my mom became much better at asking open-ended questions. She would ask, "What was the best part of your day," or, "What one thing did you learn in math class?" Her questions would draw out answers, even from a teenager, because they were more open-ended.

There are some tips to consider on how to best ask open-ended questions that will be beneficial to starting a dialogue with your customers when they don't seem to want to talk too much.

Research the Customer

First, you must be willing to take the time to study your customer. Learn about their industry and who they compete against, and talk with people who have worked with them, past or present, to get additional insights. Just like you would ask a friend's opinion on a particular store or movie, you should be doing similar research for your customer. Keep in mind this research stage is ongoing, so your questions need to remain relevant as you continue to gather insights from the customer during your sessions.

Research the Industry

Next, even if you have been in the industry for a long time, you must stay up to date on market trends and topics. This knowledge is critical because industries are constantly changing, and new trends and topics that can be discussed are emerging. Even minimally, asking your customers about the trends and topics will bring you credibility since you are aware of what they are working through.

A good way to start is to think about how you are going to bring value through your questions. This could look like staying current on market conditions, understanding competitive movement, or gathering information on upcoming regulations. Remember, you don't have to be an expert right away, but you should know how the industry operates. You should look for successful companies and see how they navigate the industry and learn any tips and pearls of wisdom you can ask about to share with other companies.

Research the Competition

Do you know who you sell against? Probably. Better yet, do you know who your customer is competing against? This shift in mindset of focusing on your customer's competition versus your own competition will help you be a true resource to your customer. You will be able to bring value because of your knowledge of their business, not just your own.

As you look to craft open-ended questions, you can use your knowledge of both your competition and the customer's competition to differentiate yourself.

Do you know where your competition struggles? Do you know where your products or services are similar? Are you selling something that is an industry disruptor or a commodity product?

What about for your customer? Are they unique in their market, industry, or what they provide? Are they struggling to service or provide something where your product or service could help? Do they provide a service that is similar to others or unique? Are they large or small? Established or start-up? Are they competing with a big business or an agile new entrant?

As you invest time and effort into understanding and researching your own competition to differentiate your benefits, it's equally important—if not more so— to dedicate a similar amount of time to researching your customer's competition. This allows you to gain insights into their challenges and needs and will help you *love* sales and ask strong open-ended questions that will create great dialogue.

A neat side effect of this research? You will get a little better each time you learn (little win), and the more you know, the more confident you will feel! This sounds like a true win-win to me!

THE 5 W'S AND H: WHO, WHAT, WHERE, WHEN, WHY, AND HOW

Earlier in the chapter, we talked about close-ended questions that lead to a response of "Yes" or "No." Now, let's look at some opening phrases that will help lead to a more open dialogue with the customer. These opening phrases are ones you probably learned in grade school—who, what, when, where, why, and how. They are the foundation for starting to craft open-ended questions. Let's look at each quickly.

Who Questions

These types of questions help to identify key decision-makers within a potential customer's organization. They can also help you understand the individuals responsible for various actions within the account (i.e., purchasing, inventory, sales, marketing, engineering, operations, etc.) You will need to determine which departments primarily help in your specific selling process and then leverage who questions to understand the right person to build a relationship with to get closer to a sale.

EXAMPLES:

- Who should I speak with to get this product on contract?
- Who would be the best person to leverage this service?
- Who else have you considered as part of your RFP process?

What Questions

These types of questions help assist sales consultants in uncovering the specific challenges or needs that the client is facing. Leveraging these types of questions helps you to tailor your product or service to the person who can buy and address their issues specifically. These openings can also help you learn more information about your product or service so that you can uncover obstacles or objections you may face later in the sales process.

EXAMPLES:

- What type of patient do you think would be the best for this product/service?
- What challenges are you having with _____?
- What would you like to do differently if time and obstacles were not a factor?

When Questions

These types of questions are more about timing and deadlines. They can help you understand the urgency of a trial or decision process. These questions can also help you understand how important certain things are to your customers by the speed with which they answer or commit to meeting again. You can leverage these questions to inquire about timing and deadlines to determine the urgency of when the customer will be making a purchasing decision.

EXAMPLE:

- When can we meet again?
- When are you planning to make a decision on next steps?
- When you are working on _____, what do you notice?

Where Questions

These types of questions are less common in sales. You may consider using these questions to inquire about where a product or service could be used physically. Or you may think about how a product or service could be used within a particular function of the business for your customer. This is not a bad phrase to start a question with; the answer will just be more specific because of the nature of the question.

EXAMPLE:

- Where would you see the implementation of Product A/Service A/Idea A be successful?
- Where should I be focusing within your business based on the [need] identified?
- Where would you spend your funds/time if there was no limit to your resources?

Why Questions

These types of questions can sometimes be seen as abrasive to customers if used in rapid succession or if they call out the customer and their choice. They are good at understanding motives, reasons, or causes behind actions or events, but be cautious of the number of times you use them. You may consider using the other question types to accomplish the same goal without asking why repeatedly. (Think of a five-year-old in a checkout line asking why he or she cannot have candy over and over again. This is not your intended goal with your customer!)

EXAMPLE

- Why are you hesitant to move forward with product A or service B?
- Why are you considering a change from what you are currently using?
- Why are you seeing a decrease in _____ more recently?

How Questions

These types of questions soften a why question but still help you to understand more about the customer. You can learn about processes, improvement areas, efficiencies, what the customer values, and more. Practice getting good at asking how questions, and you will spark great dialogue with your customers.

EXAMPLE

- How do you see _____ impacting your _____ with your customers?
- How are you currently working through _____?
- How does this solution sound to you?

You now have 18 questions that you can begin to use to practice asking open-ended questions. The key word here is practice. The skill of asking open-ended questions is to develop your own and practice them. Daily. Try asking the question and see how the customer responds. Did it help you get closer to your goals and provide value to your customer? Listen carefully to what you uncover through asking these questions and what you can learn from your customers that you can take into other sales conversations.

If you keep hearing the same response to a question you are asking, consider developing a strong, open-ended follow-up question to build upon that common response that will create even more dialogue with your customer. If you use these starter words and keep your questions focused on the customer, you will learn to *love* sales from the interactions and success you will have.

AVOIDING LEADING OR BIASED QUESTIONS

We all have biases. Part of emotional intelligence is to be aware of our biases so that we don't have them influence our customers negatively. This is very true when asking questions, too, as there are such things as leading or biased questions.

Most of the time, your customer, as a savvy consumer, will see right through these types of questions—and you do, too. They sound disingenuous, and they are. They are also stereotypical sales representative questions that would be asked when the focus is only on the sales representative and his or her profit.

They are very self-focused and can use fear tactics to make a sale. Scaring a customer into buying— outside of something that would save their life if they did not do it—is not a good tactic. Also, thinking only of achieving your quota will not feel great to your customers.

Think of your last telemarketer or direct message solicitation on social media. Did that solicitation really sound like it would benefit you, or would it benefit the person asking it?

Be cautious to ask non-biased questions that focus on the value for the customer.

Let's look at a few examples of leading or biased questions:

1. You wouldn't want to miss out on this incredible deal, would you?
2. Wouldn't you agree that our service is far superior to our competitor's?
3. Isn't it true that our product is the best fit for your needs?
4. Everyone else in your industry is moving to this new _____, why aren't you?
5. If you don't act now, there is no guarantee that _____ will still be available and we wouldn't want that, right?

As you can tell, each of these puts the customer in a very challenging spot by having to sift through the salesperson's inherent bias or leading question. Just like you, the customer is much more likely to give you a "no" response to these types of questions. Even worse, they may buy, feel regret, and then return the item (if possible) or tell everyone never to buy from that person or company again due to the bad experience they had. Practice removing bias and leading questions from your repertoire.

Active Listening and Follow-Up Questions

I love the story about a man and his wife in their house. The man goes to the doctor and says that his wife never listens to him. The doctor tells the man to go home and begin asking his wife the same question over and over until she answers him.

The man diligently goes home and asks his wife, "Hon, what is for dinner?" No response. Typical, he thinks, so he continues through the house and then asks her again, "Hon, what is for dinner?" Again, no response. He must find her now, so he moves even further into the house, and when he sees his wife, he says, "Hon, what is for dinner?" She responds, "For the third time, I said meatloaf!"

Sometimes, we think the customer is not listening to us, but really, how well are we listening to the customer?

Outside of asking questions, your ability to really listen to the answer from your customer is what will set you apart from other consultants. Your listening ability will help you *love* sales because the customer, with the right questions, will tell you what they need, and then you can help them.

As Stephen Covey says, "The biggest communication problem is we do not listen to understand. We listen to reply" (Rice 2019). If you are thinking in the background about all of the additional questions you want to ask, or how to overcome that objection, or are just plain distracted, you will not hear the customer. You are too busy ready to defend or question the customer. To help you focus on what the customer is saying and to listen to truly understand, you should use active listening.

THE ROLE OF ACTIVE LISTENING IN SALES

The 80/20 rule is leveraged in lots of different scenarios. Some people describe that 20% of the people do 80% of the work. Others say that 80% of sales come from 20% of the customers. I like to think of 80/20 as it relates to listening in sales. The customer should be talking 80% of the time, while you, as the sales consultant, should be listening or asking good questions 20% of the time.

If the customer has a need and can talk through it with you without you interrupting, what can happen? The customer can identify through your questions some areas they may not have realized were as big of an issue. The customer, if they say their need out loud, is much more likely to act on it compared to if you tell them to do it.

As humans, we like to come up with our own ideas. We do not like to be told what to do or how to do it. If this is the case, why as sales consultants are we telling our customers what to do? We should want our customers to inform us about their needs and work together with them to come up with a mutually beneficial solution.

This is where active listening comes in. Notice it says *active* not *passive* listening. Why distinguish between the two? Active can be described as alert or lively, whereas passive allows what happens without resistance.

Have you ever found yourself casually listening to a conversation? What message do you think that sends to the person you're supposed to be listening to? It's likely you didn't come across as very engaged. Perhaps you were playing a video game or on a device while the other person was talking. Maybe you weren't even looking at them, or if you were, you were daydreaming about something else, completely missing the story being told. While you may have heard words, it probably didn't result in strong engagement with the speaker.

What about when you are intently listening to a story a friend is telling you to hear the outcome because you are riveted by the plot? You would be making good eye contact, nodding, and maybe even using gestures to show your engagement. You could be sitting at the end of your seat. You would not be on any other devices because you would not want to be distracted and miss something that was said. You would tune out any distractions that could make you miss this story. That friend would know you are all-in listening to them.

If you are only asking questions to check a box or trying to elicit a certain response, guess what? Your customer knows.

However, if you ask genuine, open-ended questions focused on them and then truly listen to the answer while maintaining eye contact and using non-verbal cues like nods or smiles, your customer will know you are paying attention. Just like how you would connect with a friend telling a good story, you should connect the same way with your customers and work on being alert to their words and lively in your response to them.

Active listening is challenging. The best way to get better is to practice. First, you must stop long enough to listen to someone else so that you can actually practice listening. I have an exercise for you. Go up to a friend or loved one and ask them to tell you a random story for three minutes. During that time, you cannot interrupt or ask any questions, you just have to listen. At the end of the three minutes, you need to repeat back to your friend or loved one what you heard in the story. Next, find another person and do the same exercise. Keep practicing this with as many people as possible. As you get better at listening, at the end of three minutes, ask a great follow-up question to what you just heard.

This exercise will help you practice your listening skills so that when you are with a customer, you are better able to actually listen. As you progress to asking follow-up questions, you are actually showing the customer you heard, *and* you are able to respond to what they said with something of value. If you do not practice active listening, you will struggle to *love* sales.

DEVELOPING FOLLOW-UP QUESTIONS

Great, you've listened, but now what? Where do you go next? Close the deal? Present your product? No!

It's time to ask a follow-up question. Follow-up questions keep the conversation flowing. Just like when you are talking with a friend, you will likely ask questions naturally to want to understand more. Katherine Hampsten, in her TED-Ed talk on "How miscommunication happens," gives a great example of how to keep a conversation going (Ted-Ed 2016).

Scan to watch

Katherine describes a conversation as throwing a lump of clay back and forth. Each person catches it and then shapes the clay to fit their own unique perceptions about the conversation. The perceptions the other person uses are influenced by multiple factors, including ethnicity, religion, family background, and more. The clay is continually reworked, reshaped, and always changing. This is the same with your customers. To keep the conversation going, you need to adapt to what the customer wants to talk about and follow up with specific questions based on the lump of clay formation the customer has thrown at you.

Your ability to listen to your customer and ask appropriate follow-up questions within the normal course of conversation will demonstrate your commitment to understanding your customer's needs.

Follow-up questions can focus on a variety of topics. Sometimes, you will need to dive deeper into a specific area for further understanding. You may need clarification on the words or situation your customer is describing. You may want to unpack a particular phrase or idea that the customer shared.

As you get more experienced in asking open-ended questions, you are going to be able to better understand your customer's comments or objections. Having this knowledge will allow you to prepare potential open-ended follow-up questions that you can ask so that you are not caught off guard by the customer. Ultimately, even if you have not prepared follow-up questions in advance, the goal is to show that you are actively listening to the customer and that you are curious to know more about what they are saying.

It's important to be aware of the potential pitfalls with follow-up questions. They can sound very similar to "why" questions. If you ask too many follow-up questions, you can be perceived as pestering or just trying to keep the conversation going when there is no perceived value exchange happening. You must be intentional to listen and be mindful of when to stop asking follow-up questions and move the conversation in a new direction.

I have watched many new sales consultants get caught in the "one-track mind" scenario. They start the conversation with a good question, and then the customer answers in a way that they did not expect. Instead of being curious to know more about why the customer went in this direction, the sales consultant asks a question about his or her product or service to try to get the customer "back on track." Be mindful to let the customer direct the conversation with some solid open-ended questions for you to uncover needs and challenges, and you will be consultative. If you try to keep on your "talk track," you will likely lose the interest of the customer and *hate* the sales process.

Be Continually Curious

My children *love* watching the TV show, *Curious George*. It's about a little monkey who is curious about his world and gets himself in some funny and challenging situations due to his curiosity. I *love* that the premise of the show is about remaining continually curious.

- If you already "know" what the customer needs, why are you talking with them?
- If you already "know" when and how they are going to buy, why are you wasting your time?
- If you already "know" the people to talk with, why are you not already talking with them?

Curiosity helps us to showcase our vulnerability and our need for help in the sales process.

If each customer is truly unique, then you need to be curious about what would be best for that specific customer and not treat them as a generic customer. Consider using "I'm curious..." before you ask your question. This subtle phrase can help put your audience at ease since you are not telling or pressuring them into something, you are just curious about them or their process.

There are many ways to cultivate curiosity, but it starts with wanting to know more. Watch any three-year-old in a store, and you can learn what curiosity looks like. My son asked a ton of questions when we were out and about. Why is that person looking at that? Why is she wearing that? Why does that man have glasses? Why is he so tall? Why can't we go see toys? Why are you getting that? Why are all the people wearing green? Why are your eyes brown? Why is the sky blue? Why is the car black?

As a child, you were naturally curious about the world. You either had people in your life who continued to support that curiosity or who squashed it. I promise you, your curiosity is down inside of you, but you are going to have to go down into yourself and look for it. After you embrace the fact that you can be curious, you are going to need to start practicing using your curiosity again. Deliberately look at the world from a new perspective. Be intentional about asking curious questions. The more you practice it, the more curious you will become.

How Much Do You LOVE Open-Ended Questions?

I hope you *love* asking open-ended questions. These questions can lead to deeper customer relationships and more valuable customer insights, helping to overcome objections and close sales. You have probably heard the common phrase, "If you don't ask, the answer is always no." Get comfortable practicing asking questions to all types of people. This will help you learn how to ask better questions, listen more effectively, and follow up more intentionally.

There is no perfect question to close the sale, but there is value in practicing and honing your question-asking skills so you can improve your customer interactions. I hope you learn to *love* asking questions and see the success and meaningfulness it can bring to your customers and you.

Questions to Consider

1. Why is it easier to ask close-ended questions?

2. How will you intentionally practice asking open-ended questions?

3. What is the potential impact on your customer of asking more open-ended questions?

4. Of the 5 W's and H, which type of question do you use most often? Which type will you try now?

5. What benefit is there to you of asking more open-ended questions?

6. What does your 80/20 for listening look like now? How are you going to adjust the percentage?

7.   How can you practice active listening?

8.   What aspect of asking open-ended questions or active listening will be most challenging for you?

9.   How will you cultivate becoming more curious?

10. Who is someone you know who is curious or asks good questions? What can you learn from him/her?

11. How do you remain truthful with your customers? What areas would cause you to stretch the truth? Why?

12. What is your "go-to" question? How did you start using it? What outcome does it provide for you?

4

V = Value

One of my most valuable experiences occurred at the autobody shop. My car needed some bodywork repair done, so I asked a trusted neighbor for a recommendation in the area. I called the company and booked an appointment with them. The check-in experience was like any other, but from then on, nothing was the same. I received a text message upon leaving the keys that my car was in good hands, and I could follow its progress through the repair process online. What?! A body shop was going to text me regular updates so I wouldn't have to call and check on it. That was new!

Over the next couple of weeks, I would get regular updates that my car was "in the body shop," "getting ready for paint," or "ready for its big reveal." Each step of the process had pictures of what the car looked like and a funny little comment about the progress it was making. Upon picking up the car, the staff was friendly, and the car looked great! It was clear what services had been performed, when I needed to arrive, and how I would pay.

Do you think I should keep this autobody shop a secret? No way! I recommend this business to every person who needs work done on their vehicle.

For me, this autobody experience proved that you can have a valuable exchange anywhere and with anyone. In sales, being able to "bring value" is a common phrase for how successful consultants earn and keep business. This phrase "bring value" feels so nebulous. For you to *love* sales, you must learn to always bring value.

The next step in the LOVE Sales Framework™ is V = Value. When thinking about sales, value lies at the heart of every single interaction. If you are not bringing value to the customer, you are not going to have long-term sustainable sales. That value to the client starts with how they "feel" about you, your products or services, and how it compares to your competitors.

Peter Ackroyd summarizes value well saying, "The value is always in the eye of the beholder. What is worthless to one person may be very important to someone else" ("A Quote from Chatterton" n.d.).

In this chapter, we'll explore the value proposition, understanding your product/service and customers, demonstrating the value of what you offer, and overcoming objections.

Understanding the Value Proposition

Think of a highly valuable interaction you had with a company or someone. What did that experience look like? Now, think of a poor interaction you had with a company or someone. What did that poor experience look like? What was the main difference between the two?

For the non-valuable experience, how important did you or your problem feel? Probably not very much. Did the salesperson or company make you feel just like every other customer? You may have even felt frustrated or ignored during the interaction. Perhaps you felt misunderstood or disappointed. It's likely you have a very emotional response when you think about this poor experience and now want to tell others to completely avoid this person or company!

Now, what about the highly valuable experience? Did you feel like you were the most important person and that your needs were being met? Did the salesperson make you feel heard and understood as you spoke? You likely have a very positive emotional response to this highly valuable experience and now want to tell others in a good way about this person or company.

There is no "easy" button that can magically be pressed to express value.

Lots of factors contribute to making something feel valuable. There could be a sentimental component, or how a person made you feel, or the experience that you received.

When you have a valuable experience at a restaurant, the person waiting on you makes you feel like you are their only customer. They seem to be one step ahead of what you are going to ask for (drink refill, bread, dessert menu) and deliver it at the perfect time. Your meal was enjoyable, memorable, and a valuable use of your time because of the interactions you had with your server.

Value is personally defined. We assign certain people value because of the impact they have on our lives. Places have value because of the way they make us feel or the memories they hold. Things have value because of where we got them or who we were with so it feels valuable to us. We will each assign value to different people, places, or things due to our unique and personal experience with them.

WHAT MAKES YOU UNIQUE?

Defining what motivates you, inspires you, or causes you to go above and beyond is, at its core, your "why." If you have not yet defined your "why," you will struggle to help others define why they should work with you, buy your product or service, or listen to your idea. We'll talk more about how to find and leverage your "why" in later chapters.

You are the most valuable asset in a sales situation. The way you think, ask, and service your customer is what will set you apart from every other consultant. What about you is unique? How do you define the level of service you want to bring? What knowledge do you have, or can you gain, to be valuable to your customers?

You will have your own unique style of how to sell. The way you ask questions, your sense of humor, your drive, passion, and ambitions.

Do not try to be someone you are not—be you.

When I was practicing to become certified as an executive coach, I had to participate in mentor coaching sessions. This is where you coach for 20 minutes and then are critiqued for 10 minutes by a certified mentor coach who listened to the session. You would then switch and become the client for 20 minutes, and the other coach would have the opportunity to practice.

During my first few sessions, the mentor coach would ask me if the questions I was asking the client were my own questions or ones that I had heard someone else use. I didn't understand at first why they would even ask if they were my own questions. However, my mentor coach knew that for me to be successful and bring value, I needed to sound authentic and ask my own questions. When I tried to use someone else's model, I sounded robotic and earned the nickname Mr. Roboto.

After a few more sessions, I embraced my own authentic style of asking questions. My end goal of helping the client remained the same, but the way I achieved it was by embracing my unique skills to maximize the value I was providing to the client during the coaching session. No more Mr. Roboto!

DEFINE YOUR VALUE PROPOSITIONS

What makes your product, service, or idea valuable? What problems does it solve for your customers? This is not just the marketing messaging you receive. As you are selling to your customers, you should be looking for all the ways that your product, service, or idea will help them. When you talk with your current customers, you should be listening to the value that they say your product or service has. This research and curiosity will then help you ask better questions to uncover even more useful areas and needs for your customers.

One of the quickest ways to *hate* sales is to not *love* your product or service. If you do not truly believe in what you are selling, how are you going to be able to convince someone else to buy it?

Early in my career, I went to a job interview, and there were over 20 other people in the same room. Upon arriving, I was handed a packet and told how "great" the product I would be selling over the phone would be for customers. I would be successful if I just kept picking up that phone and calling as many friends as possible who could buy their product.

The value proposition for this company? My contacts. Their product was nothing special, but they were leveraging all those people for their personal relationships to get them sales. That is a quick way to *hate* sales.

I had another interview where the company told me I would be just like a doctor because I would work directly with the patient. I would have the same hours as the doctor, and I would be in the clinic and operating room with them. I was told I would make a ton of money, too. On the surface, this sounds like a highly valuable position.

However, I chose to dig deeper for me. This job did not align with my personal why in any way. I did not want to miss out on family time or have the pressure of being a doctor. (I could already picture the liability of making a mistake and the doctor putting the blame on me.)

You must be aligned with the value proposition for the product or service you sell. If you are not, you will not show up with your customers authentically. You will not enjoy the activities you need to do to be successful. You will be frustrated by why you are not making money and not converting customers. If you sell a product or service that you are passionate about and that aligns with your why, you will *love* sales.

As I mentioned in an earlier chapter, I chose medical device sales because of the personal impact the healthcare world had on me as a child. I wanted to help people. On the first day of a new job, a fellow sales consultant came up to me as "the new guy" and said, "Come see the piece of shit we sell." It was clear he did not believe in the value proposition of that product. However, I used that same product to win Sales Consultant of the Year by finding where it did have value for my customers.

Don't let someone else define your value or the value of your product. Discover that value for yourself.

SEGMENTING YOUR AUDIENCE

My customers in northern New England were different from my Southern New England customers, who were different from my New York customers. Even in each of these areas, the customers were unique. When I made sales calls in Southern CT, I had three different customers in the same town. One was a large, nationally known health system, another was the local hospital that was less nationally known, and the third was a government-run facility.

When I called on each of these customers, my approach was different. Each customer had the end goal of the patient in mind, but each customer approached how they cared for the patient differently. Each facility had a different way of evaluating products and making purchasing decisions. There were different rules and processes for the implementation of biomaterials that had to be followed to be considered in each system.

To be successful at each, I needed to know what would be valuable for each of these customers, not generically. I needed to know:

- which facility would be hyper-focused on clinical outcomes
- which facility that would be most concerned about who was on contract

- which facility would be most cost-focused
- which facility had the most appropriate patient population for my product.

Each of these facilities had specific needs and challenges. It was my job to uncover these needs and challenges through the questions I asked and the research I did and then align those to the value I could provide.

If you treat each customer as unique, you will *love* how your customer responds to the value proposition you deliver to them. Hint: it will be personalized and not generic. It will focus on them and their needs—not yours.

COMPETITIVE ANALYSIS

I often ask people why they use a particular cell phone or mobile carrier. I have found there is a deep loyalty to a particular brand or carrier, which is hard to logically explain. I then ask them what it would take for them to switch brands or carriers. This certainly sparks some good discussion, with both sides trying to convince the other why their brand is better.

The same is true of your customers. They already use particular products and have a reason for doing so. That reason may not be profound but could sound something like "because we always have," or logical like, "I used this product at another company, and it worked great."

Your customer will define the value of your product or service in relation to what they are already using—your competition.

Your competition may have more or fewer offerings than you. They may be more or less expensive. They may be more or less well-known in the industry.

This is precisely why you need to look for the value for the customer. If your customer is focused on having the most up-to-date technology and you work for a small, nimble company, you may have the most value and could beat much larger companies. If your customer is looking for an established, well-connected brand that has been around for a long time and you sell for that company, you can leverage that value.

If you are not researching your competition, you are going to miss areas where you can provide value because of your lack of knowledge. In *The Art of War*, Sun Tzu has a great quote about going to war that relates to understanding your competition:

> *"If you know your enemy and yourself, you need not fear the result of a hundred battles. If you know yourself and not the enemy, for every victory gained you will also suffer a defeat. If you know neither the enemy nor yourself, you will succumb in every battle."*

Each battle is for a customer against your competitor. You either get the sale (win) or do not get the sale (lose) compared to your competitor. Knowing who you are going into battle against will help you *love* sales and the value you will provide.

Identifying Customer Needs and Pain Points

I NEED this ice cream. I NEED that new toy. I NEED that equipment. As children (and, at times, adults), we often confuse a need and a want. We want ice cream, toys, and equipment, yet we rarely need them. Getting to the heart of a true need and not just a want will help you deliver value to your customers. Your ability to ask great questions, identify what's a true need, and craft a smart solution will help you deliver value.

EFFECTIVE QUESTIONING

In Chapter 3, we spoke about the importance of using open-ended questions to create a dialogue with your customer. Crafting and leveraging strong open-ended questions will encourage customers to share their challenges and objectives. If you use active listening to hear what they are saying (and not saying), you can find how your product or service would be valuable to them.

EMPATHY AND UNDERSTANDING

Empathy is the capacity to understand or share the feelings, thoughts, and perspectives of another person. As a sales consultant, your goal should be to build trust and rapport with customers by demonstrating that you care about their well-being and are focused on providing solutions that genuinely benefit them rather than just making the sale.

The concept of empathy is at the core of the LOVE Sales Framework™. We will talk more in Chapter 5 about the role empathy has in sales. As a Christian, I believe there are many great verses in the Bible about empathy that can apply to sales consultants. When you have *love* as the main focus of each of your interactions, this will help guide you to think more of others than yourself.

"Rejoice with those who rejoice, weep with those who weep."
Romans 12:15 (ESV)

"So whatever you wish that others would do to you, do also to them." Matthew 7:12 (ESV)

FEEDBACK LOOPS

As part of a leadership development course I did, one of the activities I was required to complete was a 360-degree assessment. This type of assessment is used to gather feedback from everyone involved in the person's life to give a full 360-degree view of them. Managers, peers, cross-functional partners, external partners, and even family/friends were invited to participate. The assessment included a variety of questions aimed at providing insight into the employee's performance across various aspects. The resulting report offered specific feedback on strengths and areas for improvement.

Feedback is a gift.

During this process, my manager would always tell me, "Feedback is a gift." She was exactly right. If people are willing to give feedback, view it as something that can make you better instead of an accusation. Having the right mindset for how to view the data will help you focus on how you can improve versus seeing just the negative.

Part of the way to *love* sales is to get feedback on what is working well and areas that could be better. Feedback can also help you be intentional about little wins. It can help you leverage where you are strong or plan where you need additional focus.

Most customers are willing to provide feedback. The responsibility falls on you as the sales consultant to actively seek this feedback. Rarely is there a 360-degree assessment of your sales performance on each account. You need to be proactive and learn from your customers what went well and if there are any areas for improvement. This feedback will help you improve blind spots or momentum stoppers earlier in the next sales process.

How do you do this? By asking relevant, open-ended questions where you are curious for true feedback on yourself, your product, your company, your follow-up, or any number of things.

As you continue to hear this feedback, you will be better able to learn where your customers see value in you, your product or service, and your company. Listen for what you can leverage to be more valuable and work to guide areas where you may not have the competitive edge but can still provide value for your next sales process.

Demonstrating the Value of Your Product or Service

When was the last time you received a handwritten note? A better question is, when was the last time you wrote a handwritten note?

Why are handwritten notes so effective? I believe it is because they are so personal. When you get a handwritten note, you know the person on the other end took the time to think out what they were going to say, find what they were going to write it on, properly prep it for delivery, and then figure out how to get it to you. Especially as technology continues to increase, the rarity of a handwritten note will draw positive attention if the content is well-thought out.

Personalization is a differentiator when it comes to sales.

You do not need to write only handwritten notes, but thinking about the value you bring and how you present that value to customers should be something you spend time curating in your mind.

Personalization can take multiple forms. It could be a handwritten note or remembering a customer's favorite drink item and bringing it. It could be applying what was uncovered when you were asking questions and bringing it up in a customer-focused presentation.

You will have to demonstrate your product or service in sales. A key component of actually selling is being able to showcase to the customer what you can offer. Just asking questions and then asking for a sale is valuable only to you—not the customer. The customer has just shared all these details with you based on your genuine interest, so fight the urge to go straight to the close.

There are times when asking questions can lead to a close, but most of the time, you will need to demonstrate something to the customer—how a product feels, works, or looks, or what you will include, such as the flow or outcomes of the service you provide.

Some people will want to buy immediately. Others will take their time. Some will want to hear all about what other people have to say about your product, service, or idea. Some will want every single piece of information on the company, product, features, or more. Others will want to try it before they buy while some will want to customize it.

Just like you are unique, your customer is unique. Each of them will have different needs and preferences on how they want to see the value demonstrated. In line with the handwritten note, consider three ways you can demonstrate value.

CUSTOMER-FOCUSED PRESENTATIONS

PowerPoint is pretty much a ubiquitous tool for sharing and presenting information. However, to leverage PowerPoint correctly, you need to make sure what you are showing is how your product or service will bring value to your customer. Make sure the value is clear for your customer when you are presenting, or they will not connect the value to what you are showing.

Similar to PowerPoint, if you are doing a hands-on demo, make sure the customer is at the center of the conversation. If there is a feature that you think is really nice but your customer does not have an interest in it—move on. Make your product or service demonstration about what will bring the most value to your customer, not you.

When you have developed a champion or advocate within your target customer's organization, ask them about the most effective way to present to their company. Working closely within their company provides invaluable insights into successful presentations. Allow your customer to guide you; their genuine interest in your product can give you the inside scoop on what would be the most valuable for them.

SUCCESS STORIES

For those customers who like to know "who else is using it," your ability to leverage stories will make your demonstrations much more effective. The ability to tell a good story, especially about other customers using your product, can set you apart from your competition.

In the *Harvard Business Review* article *Storytelling That Drives Bold Change*, the authors say that "Research has shown that storytelling has a remarkable ability to connect people and inspire them to take action" (Frei and Morriss 2023) They lay out a clear guide on the best way to effectively leverage the power of storytelling through four steps:

1. Understand your story so well you can describe it in simple terms.
2. Honor the past.
3. Articulate a mandate for change.
4. Lay out a rigorous and optimistic path forward.

If you have the ability to leverage video testimonials from your customers discussing the value that you, your product or service, or your company provided them, it is absolute gold.

As a sales consultant, I would meet with my customers and tell them the features and benefits. When my manager would come into town, he would tell the customer about the same features and benefits, and the customer would move forward. Did this make me a poor sales consultant? No! I learned to leverage my sales leadership team to help me move sales forward through their ability to tell stories about other prominent customers in their region. This would help the customer quantify the value that my products would provide.

The higher the level of management you bring with you on a sales call, the more they can speak about what is happening within the organization. If you have a large national customer who wants to know what other large national customers are using your products, you may need to bring in a Sales Director or Vice President who can validate the success your company and product/service is having with those large national customers. Part of your success will be to make sure your senior leader understands the goal with the customer and how they can best help you in the sales process.

Think about you personally. What type of stories do you like to hear when making a purchasing decision? When you go to upgrade to the newest phone, service, or product, who do you ask? You might not ask anyone, but do you look around? Do you research or read testimonials online? Do you trust a significant person in your life, or look to a celebrity who uses that product?

Just like you, your customer wants to hear from other customers to know that what they are buying is not going to be a dud. They want confidence that you can deliver the value you have promised and that you have delivered to other customers satisfactorily.

PRODUCT KNOWLEDGE

Become an expert. Study your products. Study your competitor's products. Study your industry. The more knowledge that you have and can bring to the conversation, the more valuable you are to the customer.

I have a lot of friends who cover surgical cases in the operating room with orthopedic surgeons. They watch multiple cases each day from multiple surgeons, so they see many different injuries and many different ways to repair them.

Over time, they become increasingly aware of what types of complications will occur in different types of procedures. They know their own products, as well as their competitor's products, and what is stocked at the hospital. They anticipate what the doctor will need next in the case and work with the scrub tech to have it available for them. The doctor keeps that sales consultant in their room because they bring value to their operating room and help improve the value they can deliver to their patients.

My friends did not become experts overnight. They spent hours, months, and years listening, watching, reading, and studying to become the valued consultants they are in the operating room. To *love* sales, you must embrace the long journey of delivering value for your customers through your increase in knowledge.

Overcoming Objections with Value-Based Selling

Objections are good. What?!

Yes, they are a sign that your buyer is still interested and willing to talk with you. If your customer is asking you what it costs, you have at least piqued their interest enough for them to consider the cost. If you have not asked enough open-ended questions to understand the gap they have in their needs, you will struggle to fill the distance between the perceived value of your product and what they are willing to pay.

What if I told you that my product costs $10,000. Do you want to buy it? Initially, that is a lot of money. But what if I was able to help show you how my product could generate $100,000 in revenue for you? That $10,000 doesn't seem as high of an investment now, does it? Investing 10% of my funds may even sound like a deal to generate $100K in revenue!

How does this relate to value? Remember that objections are a natural part of selling and that you should expect them throughout the entire sales process. If you understand the true value of your product, service, or idea, you should be able to overcome the objections more effectively. If you overcome your customer's objections, you are going to *love* sales because you are about to get an order! Let's look at some ways to *love* handling objections.

OBJECTION ANTICIPATION

If you have been actively selling to your customers, you should have a list of common objections you have heard, such as your product is too clunky or your service is too slow. I can pretty much guarantee you have heard that your price is too high!

By anticipating your customer's potential objections, you will be better prepared to respond to them effectively. This allows you to turn their objections from negatives into value statements.

This turnaround may sound something like this: "I have had other customers tell me my product looks clunky, but my current customers actually like the boxier feel because it has a better fit in their hands."

The turnaround may also sound something like this: "I realize you may perceive our service as slow, but we take extra care to make sure that our initial release is correct so that we don't have to work through any glitches upon installation and can get you up-to-speed more efficiently."

Being willing to acknowledge that you are going to get objections and anticipating them will make you feel more in control of the sales call.

If you know that your customers normally mention an objection during your process, you can be proactive in addressing it and then share how other current customers feel about it. This will show the customer that you are aware of the objection, have dealt with this type of situation in the past and that it has been handled effectively. This will increase trust in you and your product or service with the customer so the objection doesn't feel so overwhelming.

VALUE REINFORCEMENT

If you have not asked enough open-ended questions to uncover your customer's true needs, you will struggle to reinforce your value because simple objections can derail your value reinforcement. Be prepared to always listen to what the customer is saying because even in an objection, they may help you understand the value that your product, service, or idea could bring.

What do I mean? Let's consider an example:

CUSTOMER: Your inventory system seems overwhelming to my staff.

CONSULTANT: I can totally understand that learning something new can feel overwhelming. What specifically do you feel is challenging for your staff?

CUSTOMER: My staff just wants to scan the items and have them done. They don't want to have to worry if the system will actually work since they have had trouble in the past.

CONSULTANT: I can understand how this peace would be a benefit for your staff. During our previous conversation, we talked about how this inventory system has a superior scanning capability, and we have a guarantee that if, for some reason, the scanner does not capture the items properly, we will make it right free of charge. I'll also be here in person during the first few weeks to train and help your staff when they are learning to use the system. This way, we can mitigate the fear of potential errors. What impact do you think these actions would have on your staff feeling overwhelmed using the new system?

Did you notice how I did not just say, "I can help you not feel overwhelmed." We need to understand what is causing the staff to feel overwhelmed. This is where follow-up questions help you get to the deeper cause of the objection. We now also know that the competitive inventory system has a scanning problem. This is something that we can build questions around during our next prospective visits to new customers.

That question may sound something like, "I'm curious, how important is the accuracy of scanning to you and your staff when evaluating an inventory system?"

Objections provide an opportunity to reinforce why the customer has expressed interest in your product already. Let your responses help to build upon the established need you have identified and reinforce the value you will bring to your customer.

HANDLING PRICE OBJECTIONS

Price is the most common objection you will get in sales. Every sales consultant will hear, "Your price is too high." There are many reasons for price objections.

I had a pastor who once told me that "anger is a secondary emotion." As he described it to me, it means that you can be angry, but you are not just angry to be angry. There is something that is bothering you, an underlying issue, which is causing you to feel angry.

The same is true of price objections—price objections are a secondary emotion. The customer is interested enough in your product or service to ask what it costs (good job!), but there is an underlying issue that they have yet to raise or solve that you may or may not know about. Depending on the size of that underlying issue depends on the price of your product.

For example, if you have a flat tire and someone offers to fix it for $200, you may think that is high but will go with it because of the situation you are in. However, if you have decent tread on your tire and are not actively looking for a new tire, you may consider $200 to be outrageous. Our view of price depends on the underlying emotions we are feeling, the weight difference between price and value, and our current situation.

Higher price without
enough value ≠ sale

Higher price with
higher value = sale

To *love* sales, you must embrace talking about price. If you feel that the value you bring collectively (yourself, your product, your company) is worth what you are offering to the customer to help them, then you should feel confident in having the price conversation.

I always told my customers that I would not be offering them this price if I did not think my product or service would bring them more value than they paid for it. The value to the customer could also take a long time to be realized. Helping the customer understand what they are paying for and the overall value impact is important throughout the pricing conversation.

For example, I sold a stationary device compared to a competitive handheld device. The handheld device was more portable (obviously), but the replenishment cost was much higher than my device. During the negotiation stage, after I had asked lots of questions to determine if my product was a good fit for the customer, I would provide a cost analysis for the customer using their data. This analysis would show the short-term cost per patient for both my device and the handheld device.

The graph would show as the number of samples the customer used per day increased, the more price advantageous my device became. The graph would demonstrate to the customer they would save significant money in the long term by switching to my product.

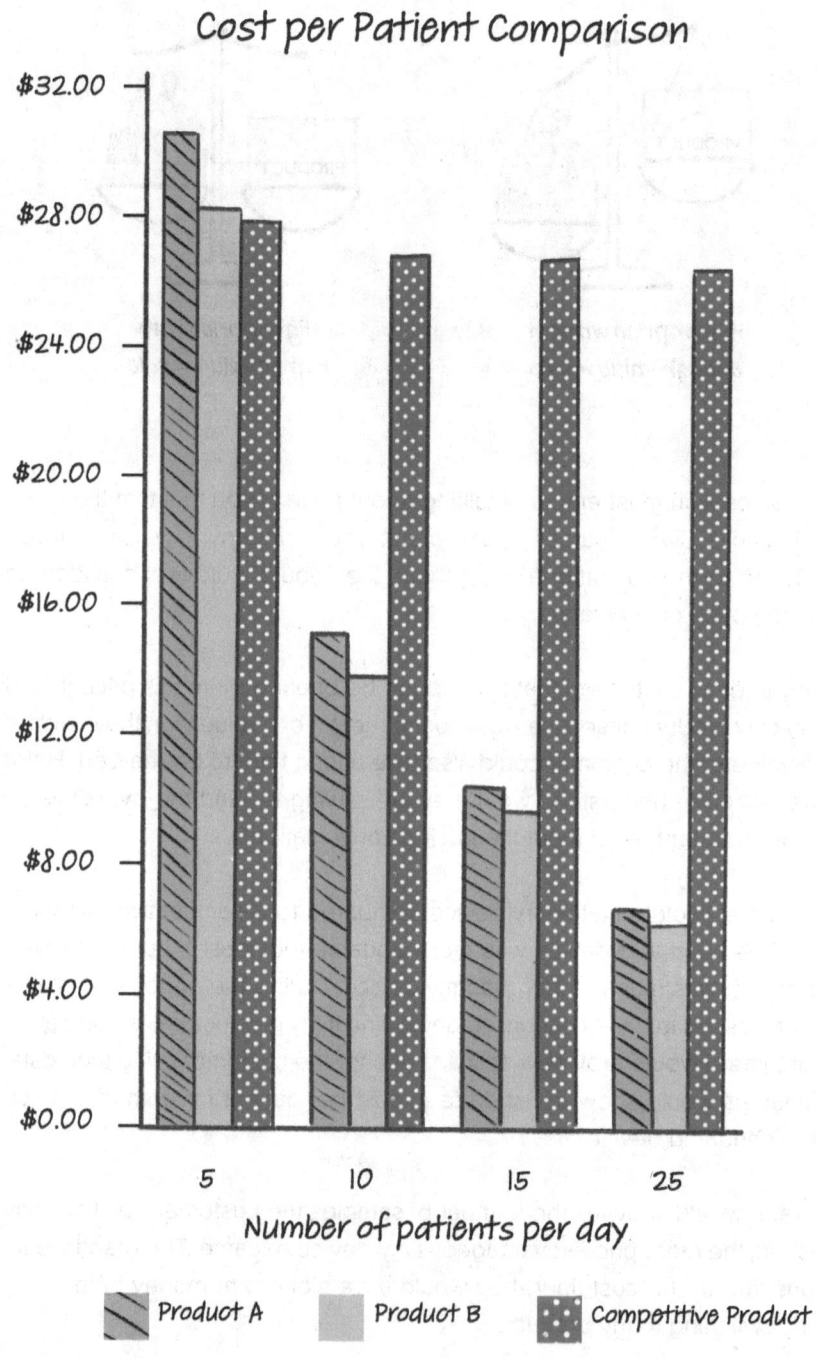

Cost per Patient Comparison

Getting the customer to realize that their guaranteed price may not show immediate results requires embracing the pricing conversation. The longer it takes to get to the breakeven of what they are currently using or switching from, the harder it is to overcome a price objection. You must leverage strong questions and customer champions to effectively overcome price objections.

"People don't like to be sold, but they love to buy."
JEFFREY GITOMER (GITOMER 2017).

The Value in The LOVE Sales Framework™ is a word that often gets overused and misunderstood. However, if you put your customers first, serve them with *love*, and think about how your product or service helps them meet their needs, you can be successful and *love* sales. Embrace objections as insight into your customers' heads and what they are most concerned about to move forward. Keep practicing, learning, and clarifying, and you will become a valuable resource for your customers. Be confident in yourself, your product or service, and your company, and you will *love* the value you can provide to your customers.

Questions to Consider

1. What is something you consider high value? What makes it highly valuable?

2. What was one of your most valuable interactions? What made it valuable?

3. What value does your competition have? How are you alike or different?

4. When was the last time you heard a price objection? When was the last time you used a price objection? What was the motive behind each?

5. How can showing love help you be more valuable to those around you and your customers?

6. What types of stories do you gravitate towards? How can you tell these types of stories to your audience?

7. When do you focus on needs versus wants? Why?

8. How do you adapt your approach to best connect with your audience?

9. Who is someone who can give you specific and actionable feedback? How will you be intentional to get feedback from customers?

10. What three things make you unique? How can you use these attributes to bring value to your customers?

E = Emotional Connection

"Our product has been proven to be superior clinically. There is no reason the customer should not buy it." That was a comment I received from senior leaders at my company when I told them that a customer chose to buy from someone else. This person could not understand why someone would decide not to move forward with a proven, superior product.

Let me give you some background. I was selling a newer-to-market medical device, and we would conduct in-person, head-to-head studies between medical devices. The accuracy of the readings between both devices would be tested on the same sample, and then a standard deviation would show how accurate each portable device was compared to a centralized, gold-standard device.

I had worked with the customer to understand their needs. I had uncovered that accuracy was important to them in the device they used. I understood and qualified that pricing was comparable to what they were currently using or considering. The customer was willing to and did complete an in-facility head-to-head comparison between my device and a competitive device. I brought value with the demonstrations and objection handling, so the customer felt comfortable with me and my device.

When the results came in, my device had a statistically significant better standard deviation than my competitor. My device had shown a clear clinical advantage. This proved the point of the senior leader at my company that my product was superior to the competitive product. The next step was for the customer to cut a Purchase Order (PO) and for me to continue servicing the customer through implementation.

The sale never came. The customer purchased from my competitor. The same competitor who did not show clinical superiority. Wait a minute, what happened here?!

People are emotional beings. We are not robots that make decisions solely based on the most logical solution. We follow our "feelings" or "hunches" even when they are contrary to logic. This is the foundation for the next letter in the LOVE Sales Framework™—E = Emotional Connection.

My senior leaders did not understand this concept. They looked at every situation linearly. They thought that no sale should ever be lost if the data showed superiority. Their expectation was a 100% conversion rate because if the data proved the product's superiority, it "must be the sales consultant that had the issue." Fundamentally, they believed that every customer simply looked at the data, saw that the data was better, and would then be willing to pay any amount required to ensure they had the "most accurate" product.

Wrong! While the data was important to the customer, there were other factors that played a role in their decision, including the aesthetics of the device, company size they were purchasing from, relationships within the company and sales consultants, market positions of the products being compared, peer recommendations from others they trusted or went to school with, and many more factors.

To *love* sales, you have to do your best to understand all of the emotional connections that could impact your sale. Customers may not directly share this information with you, but you can uncover it by asking deeper open-ended questions that connect with customers emotionally. The questions could focus on potential risks or benefits you will be able to uncover and some of the emotional hurdles you may have to overcome.

If you worked with a sales consultant who had previously promised that they would service your account after the sale, and then they never showed up again, how would you feel? You are going to hold back emotionally when another sales consultant "promises" the same thing to you. The customer may even have a "prove it" mentality towards sales consultants, given how many times they have promised something and then never delivered it.

The more times that you hear something and it does not happen, the more you will build emotional walls, and a lack of trust grows. When you are working with customers, they have emotional walls built from previous experience working with sales consultants. To *love* sales, you must break down those pre-built walls by emotionally connecting with your customer in a way other sales consultants can't or are not willing to do.

It is important to remember that you can only control your actions and emotions, not the actions and emotions of your customers.

Therefore, it is critical to learn how to build trust and empathy with customers so that you can build those emotional connections.

Think of your personal life and those strong emotional connections you have with loved ones. Did those strong connections happen in a day, a week, a month? Certain relationships can have a quick emotional connection at first, but deep, trusting emotional connections take time and effort to build and grow. Think of something very personal to you. Would you share that something on your first date? Highly unlikely! However, you may share it with a parent, spouse, or good friend with whom you have trust, rapport, and tenure.

Give your customers time to grow in your relationship. Make sure that you treat them with respect and *love*. Consistently follow through on what you have promised. Be transparent with your advantages and challenges.

To *love* sales, you must first be able to understand and *love* yourself through an understanding of emotional intelligence.

Emotional Intelligence

Emotional intelligence is a critical factor for your success in sales. At times, it can feel like a buzzword, but there are three critical areas to remember when it comes to emotional intelligence: self-awareness, self-regulation, and empathy.

SELF-AWARENESS

Self-awareness is how well you understand your own emotions. What are your strengths and weaknesses? What are your values? How are you motivated? It is important to leverage your strengths and mitigate your weaknesses so you can build connections with your customers. Your ability to know yourself is the first step in your ability to learn to know others.

Creating an emotional connection with others must first start with knowing what is most important to you.

There are many different assessment tools available to help you better understand yourself. One of my favorites is CliftonStrengths®. It focuses on identifying and ranking people's strengths based upon 34 themes to help them build upon their natural strengths. One of my CliftonStrengths® is an achiever mindset. I feel my best when I have accomplished something meaningful each day. It needs to be more than just making my bed in the morning.

One way that I maximize my strengths is to make sure I exercise each day. This helps me physically and mentally to show up well for my family, friends, and co-workers. The workout helps to clear my mind, challenge my abilities, and make me feel good about what I have done for myself and my body. In my mind, exercise is a meaningful achievement. Days without exercise can have meaningful achievement, but it may take some work.

This achiever mindset is also one of the reasons little wins are so important in the sales process. For me, having a goal I was working towards each day helped to keep me motivated and my eye on the ultimate prize: Sales Consultant of the Year. It also helped me understand when I was not in my best state emotionally.

SELF-REGULATION

Self-regulation is all about how well you can control your emotions in various situations. This may be a reason you will NOT *love* sales because you will get put into a LOT of situations where it may be hard to control your emotions. Lots of sales advice reminds sales consultants, "They are rejecting your product, not you," but that doesn't mean it still doesn't hurt!

Your ability to know your triggers and intentionally work on them will help you overcome various situations. Learn what annoys you, delights you, challenges you, and upsets you, and you will be on the road to understanding self-regulation. I'm not going to go into details on the methods for self-regulation as there are many books on that topic, but you must work to know your triggers to regulate.

For me, I once had an appointment to do a sales call at a three-hospital system and showcase my product to a department head in the hospital. I arrived early so I could be prepared, and during my setup, some of the techs in the department came over to ask me about my product. I gladly gave them the details, and they asked me a few questions.

However, I was shocked when, as I was answering their questions, they began to laugh and point at me, telling me how stupid my product was. They couldn't believe anybody would buy this piece of junk. They found it so amusing that they immediately called their department head and proclaimed, "Boss, you've got to get out here and hear about this product. It is terrible! Quick, do your demo again; he won't believe how bad this product is. Come quick!"

I was boiling mad inside! I had wasted hours of my day driving and preparing for this appointment. Now they were making fun of my product directly to my face and telling me how terrible it was. You can already guess that I knew I wasn't likely to get this sale unless the department head had a totally different personality from his team and didn't ask for input from any of his techs. Highly unlikely. When the department head arrived, he laughed at my product, too, and found the demo amusing.

Telling myself they were rejecting my product was the easy part. Not verbally lashing out and making any negative or spiteful comments about them or their health system required extreme self-control. I kept the verses, *"do to others what you would have them do to you,"* and *"if anyone slaps you on the right cheek, turn to him the other cheek also"* (Matt 7:12 and Matt 5:39, NIV) at the top of my head.

These verses helped me to remain calm, so I was able to thank them for their time and promptly leave the facility. I did not get a call back from them to purchase my product (no surprise) or, thankfully, to perform another stand-up comedy demo show with my product.

This self-control did not happen immediately. Each sales call is an opportunity for you to practice your self-regulation:

- Did that one comment hit you the wrong way? Figure out how to move forward and remain focused on the client.
- Did the client set an appointment with you four hours away and then not show up? Find some other accounts in the area that you can call on, send a follow-up to connect at another time, and move on.
- Did your competitors badmouth you or your product to your customer? Keep your character intact by addressing anything incorrect and beating your competitors by out-servicing them.

You cannot control what others will say or do, but you can control how you respond.

Practice, practice, practice. Practice a positive, *loving* response, and you will set yourself apart from the other sales consultants in the same situations.

Learn to regulate your response. Do not be a pushover; instead, recognize the power of words and actions. Each time you are representing a product or service, you are the spokesperson for the organization and set the standard for how the customer will view your company going forward.

EMPATHY

Empathy is best described as walking in another's shoes. Your goal with empathy is to understand and share the other person's feelings. This is very easy to say and very difficult to do.

Think of someone you love dearly. How do you go about understanding their feelings? We will discuss empathy more in a little bit. In relation to emotional intelligence, empathy can help you communicate with your customers, collaborate with your team, and resolve conflicts during the sales process. Empathy also fits well into the LOVE Sales Framework™ because it focuses on others, not yourself.

Think, feel, and understand what is important to your customer, and you will *love* sales.

Building Trust and Rapport

According to Merriam-Webster, trust is the assured reliance on the character, ability, strength, or truth of someone or something. I once heard someone say, "People don't buy from people they like, they buy from people they trust." If trust is so important in sales, how can you build it with your customers to have success?

BE RESPONSIBLE

As emotional people, we value consistency when it comes to certain things. We appreciate that our car starts each morning, that our phone chargers work when plugged in, and that the refrigerator keeps our food cold. We become frustrated when these things do not work as expected.

How frustrating it is when your car won't start, and you have somewhere to be! Or when you wake up and realize that the charger did not actually charge your phone, and you have less than 10% battery heading into the day.

Just as we expect our devices and equipment to perform their expected functions day-to-day, your customers expect the same from you. If you say you will be there for a 9:00 AM appointment, be there. If you say you'll send the email, send it. If you commit to providing a proposal by the end of the week, send the proposal by the end of the week (or earlier).

Your consistent actions will build predictability and reliability, which in turn will help you cultivate trust and a deeper emotional connection with your customers.

Let me share a personal example that drives this point home. My wife and I were attending a wedding out of town, and one of my best friends from college who lived there offered to drive us to the airport early the next morning. Per usual at a wedding, we spent time late into the night partying, dancing, and having a good time. My wife kept asking me if we should just get a cab since she wasn't sure my friend was going to show up. I told her not to worry; he would be there.

I had a history with my friend. I knew he was a man of his word. He was responsible for his actions, and if he said, "I'll be there," he would be there. Sure enough, when we exited the elevator early the next morning, he was standing there with a big smile, coffee in hand, ready to take us to the airport. I trusted him, and I was confident that he would be there. Being responsible and doing what you say you will do builds trust.

BE CLEAR

I know this will probably shock you, but there is no 100% perfect product, service, or idea. While there may be some excellent products, services, or ideas, nothing is perfect, so there are going to be challenges. As a sales consultant, you have a choice to tell your potential customer about the challenges you are aware of, or you can keep it hidden to "get the sale." While both options may land you the sale, telling the customer about your benefits and potential challenges will earn you long-term trust with them.

Being clear does not mean sharing all your dirty laundry and all your secrets. As it relates to sales, be honest and upfront with the customer about what your product or service can and cannot do.

Be willing to look for and find answers to questions that you cannot answer. It is much better to say, "I don't know," than to make something up to try to sound smart. Eventually, the customer is going to figure out that you don't know what you're talking about.

Let me share with you a time when I messed up in my sales career. Once, I did not attend a meeting I set up with a customer because I saw my competitor's car in the parking lot. Yep, I sure did. It's embarrassing to admit, but it happened. I had a scheduled meeting time with my customer, but I never went in to meet with him. I missed the meeting completely. I just sat in my car and waited for my competitor to leave, which he never did, so I eventually drove away.

Now, I did come back the next day to see if my competitor's car was gone—thankfully, it was—and I went into the account. My customer was mad (rightfully so!) and proceeded to ask me why I didn't show up for our meeting. I told him that I saw that my competition was here, and I didn't come in. I was 100% honest with him and fully transparent about my mistake.

It would have been much easier to make up a grand story about another urgent matter that I had to address or pretend to be dumb and say that I forgot we had an appointment. The best part of being vulnerable and open with my customer was that he taught me a very valuable lesson after I was honest with him.

The customer told me to be confident in myself and my products, and it shouldn't matter if the competition was there or not. If I believed that I had something better to offer him than my competition, he would want me to come in and share it. Whoa! That one interaction fundamentally changed how I viewed myself as a sales consultant.

I realized I brought more value than my competition, and I could be confident that all I could control was how great my product was, not how my competition responded to me. Being open and honest helped me learn a valuable lesson, and I believe it was because of this that the customer gave me advice rather than refusing to ever see me again.

BE COMMUNICATIVE

To build trust, you must be able to communicate. Albert Mehrabian, Professor Emeritus of Psychology at UCLA, created the 7-38-55 rule to quantify how meaning is conveyed through different parts of communication ("How to Use the 7-38-55 Rule to Negotiate Effectively" 2021). The three parts he highlights are words, tone, and body language. Basically, what you say, how it sounds, and how you look while doing it.

Look at the image below. How open do you feel this person is to hear what you have to say?

Now, what about this person?

You are good! The second person looks much more approachable. Neither of them said a word, but you were still able to figure it out. This is exactly what Mehrabian uncovered. He showed that:

$$Words = 7\%$$
$$Tone\ of\ Voice = 38\%$$
$$Body\ Language = 55\%$$

Take a moment to think about this: You've worked hard on your pitch, honing the exact words you want to use, but that only accounts for 7% of your communication to the customer. If your words do not have energy or your posture is slouched, you may have the best pitch ever, but it will not be well received by your audience because 93% of communication is how you say something by your tone and body language.

This is why communication plays a critical role in building trust. It's not just about the words you say but also the tone of your voice and the way you carry yourself. Be intentional in putting your entire focus on the customer. Just because you drove three hours and then had to wait for another hour for the customer to see you, don't let that come through in your interactions. Remember, just as you can tell someone's level of interest by their body language, the customer can also tell the same about you.

To *love* sales, you must embrace all aspects of communication, not just the words that you say.

BE AUTHENTIC

"You do You" is a phrase that has been popularized for embracing being authentic. If I try to pretend to be someone else or say what I think you want to hear so that you'll buy from me, I'm not being authentic. Do I genuinely care about how my product or service will help you, or am I just making my routine calls in hopes that I can hit my number and go on the company trip this year?

Most people can feel when someone is not genuine or authentic in their interaction. The same is true of your customers. They can tell if you care more about them or about what you can get from them.

When I was asked to give a presentation the next morning after an awards dinner, I knew it needed to be memorable since people would be tired from the night before. I was presenting to over 300 sales consultants on how my education team was changing how we were delivering and monitoring training. We were no longer going to continually check to see if their work was complete, but we were going to make sure we were building great content to make them stronger. If they chose to do the work, they would learn; if they did not do the work, it wasn't our problem.

For me to show up authentically, I need to be able to have fun and think differently. Leveraging this to capture the audience's attention, I decided to dress up as a policeman and then tear off my outfit during my talk and have a workout outfit underneath. To fit the theme, I was moving our training team from being a police officer (did you do your training?) to a strength coach (how can we make you better?).

Getting on stage is challenging enough, but going on stage and officially ripping your pants off in front of your company president and other senior leaders could be grounds for an instant firing. To embrace my authentic self, I dressed up and successfully pulled off the wardrobe change on stage. The sales team and my senior leaders *loved* it! The Education Strength Coach became a personality all its own and helped to transform a culture of education and innovation.

 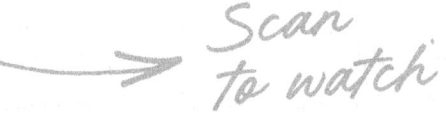

Scan to watch

Be genuine and authentic in your interactions. Customers can sense sincerity, and it forms one of the ways you can build trust with others.

Having your customers trust you will help you *love* sales.

The Role of Empathy in Sales

I was in a customer's waiting room with one of my co-workers, waiting to meet with the manager, Sean. I had been in the facility a few times before to familiarize myself with the layout and the key people. While we were waiting, a sharply dressed sales consultant arrived. He was impeccably dressed in a nice tie, pressed shirt, a blue patterned suit, and polished shoes—clearly dressed for success. Without hesitation, he approached the receptionist and asked for Sean. The receptionist kindly informed him that Sean was not available that day and suggested he come back at another time.

I looked at my co-worker. Since we were waiting to see Sean, too, why was he not available? My partner, who was local to the area, smiled and said, "Everybody in these parts doesn't trust anybody who wears a tie." It was an interesting comment, but it helped me understand the true meaning of empathy. While I felt confident in front of customers in a suit and tie, and I personally may want to dress that way for success, how I look and feel needs to make my customer feel comfortable first and foremost.

I continued to wait in my polo and khakis, and a few minutes later, Sean emerged, and we had our meeting. Because of the introduction from my co-worker and his empathic fashion reminder, I was able to connect with Sean on each of my visits and build a strong, mutually beneficial relationship with that account.

It is impossible to fully see the situation from another's point of view because of our unique experiences, but as a sales consultant, to *love* sales, you must work hard to empathize with, understand, and share the feelings of your customers. If you can develop and remain aware of this important skill, you will build a strong emotional connection and *love* sales.

Let's consider three ways to build empathy in sales:

PUT YOURSELF IN THEIR SHOES

I'm reminded of the famous quote from Harper Lee's *To Kill a Mockingbird*: "You never really understand a person until you consider things from his point of view...until you climb into his skin and walk about in it." To be successful in sales you must take into account your customers' perspective.

You need to leverage all your senses when you are with them to take in the full situation:

1. Is the environment tense because of a challenge?
2. Is the staff always playing catch up because their process is inefficient or their workload too great?
3. Are there supply issues where the customer cannot get the necessary products?
4. Is there a lot of staff or not enough staff?
5. Is it too noisy? Too quiet?
6. Does it smell clean? Dirty?

Keep in mind the ways that you can help your customer by walking in their shoes:

1. Can you help ease tension with your product or service to help smooth operations?
2. Can you help improve staff or location efficiency so that your customer can save time, money, or effort?
3. Can you improve the delivery or inventory system to streamline operations? Do you have a product that could eliminate other products to reduce the amount of inventory needed to store or track?
4. Do you have a service that can help train workers to be more effective or provide additional staffing to balance workloads?
5. Do you have a product or service that can help manage the office environment with the noise, smell, or appearance?

If you can see what your customer sees and can help them meet their goals or needs, you will be better able to emotionally connect with them.

Think of it this way: what is that customer going home and talking to his or her family about each day that drives him or her crazy? Those challenges or frustrations are the heart of the emotional challenges that need to be overcome. If you have a product or service that helps ease those challenges and you are focused on your customer and not yourself, you will *love* sales and the emotional impact you will have with them.

VALIDATE EMOTIONS

As a reminder, we are all emotional beings. We have feelings and good days and bad days. You are not a robot, and neither is your customer. Some people are much more willing to share their feelings, but remember, everyone has feelings. Plus, feelings are not all negative. We can express excitement, joy, or laughter, but we also can have frustration, uncertainty, or fear.

Whenever I got towards the close of a large deal, I always had to work with the customer to validate that it was going to be okay. Working on a large $2 million deal, my customer was feeling nervous that my company and I would not be able to support their entire system with my products. They liked the technology, and they liked my service, but they had genuine uncertainty about the full-scale rollout. I made sure to validate that this was a normal emotional response, and I assured them that other customers of equal and greater size had switched to my product and were able to be installed and serviced.

If you cannot identify or validate the emotions of your customer, you will struggle to build long-term customer relationships and value.

TAILOR SOLUTIONS

When you visit the doctor, they don't take one look at you and say, "Ah, yes, you must have a sore throat with some slight chest congestion and a rash on your lower back." If all those were true, that would be incredible, but no, your doctor uses questions to understand what is bothering you and then tailors a solution to help solve those challenges. This could include what medicine you may need, certain exercises that you need to complete, or a specialist who could help.

Just like with your doctor, having a lack of emotional awareness makes it very difficult to empathize and connect with your customer. Your end goal is to provide a meaningful solution for your customer based on the needs that you uncover. You can then be aware of the full situation so that you can tailor a solution that is a win for you and a win for your customer in the state they are in.

Let's consider my earlier example with Sean. If I had shown up in a suit and tie, Sean would still be in the office, but he would not have seen me. I had to use someone he trusted (my co-worker) and dress in a way that showed I understood his office dynamic (polo shirt versus suit). Being willing to adjust my selling, fashion, or question style to fit my customer's style conveys that I genuinely care about my customer and their well-being versus my own self-interest (i.e., make a sale to hit my quota).

How People Use Emotion to Buy

"She loves princess cut diamonds, so I'll get her those for our engagement ring."

"We love the beach, so we should take a trip to the Caribbean."

"That dog is so cute, and her hair is so soft, and she is so cuddly, I have to buy her!"

"I have to have the latest phone, or I won't look cool to all of my friends."

"I need to get a nice car, or people will think I'm poor."

We've all done it—purchased an item strictly on emotion. It's like when you finish exercising and feel good about yourself, then decide to order a milkshake from Chick-fil-A. You didn't need the milkshake as your post-workout drink, but it sure felt good!

We are emotional beings, and our decisions are often guided by emotions. Your customers make decisions the same way.

Recognizing that buying decisions are often driven by emotions can help you keep a steady focus when the sales process gets dicey, and customers start to act irrationally (which often means they are expressing their emotions). Let's explore more about how emotions drive buying decisions.

FEAR AND DESIRE

At the core, we are either seeking to avoid pain or problems, or trying to achieve our goals and find pleasure. This is where leading with *love* can be a significant advantage for you as a sales consultant.

Fear

Lots of bad sales consultants lead with or leverage fear tactics to get sales. "If you don't act today, the discount is gone!" But customers also leverage fear to tap into sales consultants' emotions: "If you don't get me a 10% discount today, I'm going to use your competitor."

As emotional beings, we are wired for human connection, and fear is a very powerful emotion. Have you ever had the "Sunday Scaries" before work on Monday? How about a job or a boss that gave you anxiety? Did you ever have a moment where you forgot where you left your phone (or something important) and couldn't find it right away? There is a feeling of panic or dread in the pit of your stomach as you try to remember where it could be!

This feeling may happen to you in sales, too. You may have it when you are trying to get the last sale of the month (or year) so you don't disappoint your manager or get called out on a team call for missing your quota. You may fear you could be fired if you end up at the bottom of the sales totem pole. You may fear that you can't eat because you haven't made any commissions.

While you may be afraid, leveraging fear to close a sale will not result in a long-term relationship with the customer. One or both of you will have distrust or unease. Your likelihood to make the sale, or any future sales, is in serious jeopardy.

In full disclosure, I tried this technique early in my career, and it did not work. Remember that point-of-care device I was selling that was so accurate? Well, I was having trouble with a customer giving me the time of day, so I decided to send an email to the CEO of the hospital telling her that her current product was killing patients.

Guess what? I ended up having a meeting with the customer in less than 48 hours. The quality team immediately set up a time with me to discuss the situation. It was nice to see the CEO was doing her job to put patient safety first in her hospital. The meeting went well, and the quality team was receptive to what I had to say regarding the situation.

Fast forward one week, and I get a phone call from my sales VP asking me if I emailed the CEO of a particular hospital. I told him yes and that I had a meeting with the quality team about a week ago. He informed me that the hospital CEO had subsequently emailed my company CEO requesting me to be fired! Whoa, that was not what I was expecting.

Evidently, the hospital staff that wouldn't see me took offense that I would go so high up in the chain to make them "look bad," so they requested my termination. Thankfully, I worked for a company that valued taking risks and believed in the efficacy of their products, so my company CEO wrote back to the hospital CEO saying we would rather lose business than one of their top sales consultants. My CEO also affirmed my position that the competitive device was dangerous for patients.

Let me ask you a question. Do you think that the hospital staff was willing to see me again? That's a total layup, no way! While I did get an appointment using a fear tactic, I never had the chance to actually sell to the customer because I was on a "blacklist" for some time whenever I entered the facility.

Hear me out. I'm all in favor of challenging customers to help them see a situation in a new way, I'm just not advocating that you use fear of a situation or outcome to accomplish this. I could have asked better questions and worked to build better connections with people at the account so that I didn't have to resort to blindly emailing the CEO and expecting her to miraculously say, "We want to buy your product!"

Desire

To sell with *love*, you must focus on what is important for the customer and what brings them joy. What do they like to talk about? What are they interested in? What are their short- or long-term goals? Focusing on customer desire is not a physical desire but an alignment with your customer's needs.

As a sales consultant, you are going to get asked by your manager, most likely monthly, "Go ask your customers for a large order so we can hit our objective." Guess what? I never did. What?! Why not?

Let's look at this question and think about the customers' needs and what they desire. Do they need to place a large order at the end of the month? (Maybe/maybe not.) Do they have a sales quota to achieve? (Maybe/maybe not.) Do they have enough stock already? (Maybe/maybe not.)

I would continually check in with my loyal customers and ask them about their needs. If they had a genuine need to fill because of increased demand or their own quota to achieve, and I could help, I would place a month-end order.

Watch most commercials and you will see a focus on desire. If you want to look rich, wear this or that. If you want to show status, drive this or that. If you want to look younger, use this or that. Marketing firms play on people's internal, emotional desires. They know that we buy based on fear or desire, which is why they use it!

However, consider for a minute if you buy a product based on desire and it does not achieve its intended purpose. How do you feel after that purchase? Frustrated! Your customer will feel the same way if you are thinking only of your own desires as the sales consultant and not of theirs. They may give you that one large order this month, but depending on how it made them feel, you may or may not get an order again.

I hear you; that is not logical, but that is the point. If you want to *love* sales, you must think through what you need to do each day to hit your objective (little wins) and then focus on what your customer needs (value) and connect with their emotions (emotional connection). This will ultimately drive enough sales that you will not need end-of-the-month sales to hit your objective, and you will build long-term customer relationships versus transactions.

> *"Wealth gained hastily will dwindle, but whoever gathers little by little will increase it."* PROVERBS 13:11 (ESV)

You must adjust your perspective to think long-term in sales versus only quick wins. As the above proverb shows, if you use fear or desire to gain wealth, you will lose it, but over time, and sale by sale, you will see an increase in your wealth.

One of my favorite verses is: *"The plans of the diligent lead surely to abundance, but everyone who is hasty comes only to poverty."* Proverbs 21:5 (ESV). In sales, if you are willing to plan and put in hard work, it will lead to abundance. But if you only focus on a quick sale, not the customer's emotion, you will struggle to build long-term wealth. You must be committed to the long haul to help your customers achieve their desires, and you will *love* sales!

STORYTELLING

Stories captivate us. When was the last time you saw a good movie, read a good book, or heard a good story around the campfire? Why do you think it was good? Did you like the characters, plot, or setting? Maybe it helped you escape your reality for a little bit and took you to a new place.

Stories evoke a lot of emotions in us. They can make us cheer. They can make us cry. They can make us feel mad. They can make us laugh.

Guess what? Your customers **love** *stories, too.*

To *love* sales, you have to *love* telling a good story. It will be hard to sell an idea if your story is not compelling. *Shark Tank* is a reality TV show where business owners present their ideas to five sharks (potential investors), and then each shark decides if they are going to invest in the business or if they are "out." Each concept being presented on the show starts with a story about how the product, service, or idea came to be and how it is impacting people.

To get good at telling various stories, you must realize what types of story-telling are relevant to connect with your audience emotionally. You must also not embellish the truth in your story to hype your solution to more than it can possibly achieve. Let's explore a few ways you can *love* sales by telling stories.

Success Stories

Just like any good book, a relevant story needs to have a good plot and struc-ture. A five-stage story structure could look something like this:

1. **Conflict/Objection:** What does the prospective customer not like about your product/service?
2. **Rising Action:** What impact does that conflict/objection have on a pro-spective customer buying your product/service?

3. **Climax:** Have other prospective customers experienced this same thing with your product/service?

4. **Falling Action:** How do current customers respond positively to the objection?

5. **Resolution:** What is the positive impact on the current customer now that they are using your product/service for the prospective customer? (Abraham, Jr. 2023)

Your ability to share a good story around a common objection will help your prospective customer to be more willing to move forward. That story may ease their concerns, provide some additional context, or raise additional questions.

I used to do training sessions with nurses at hospitals of all sizes. A common complaint I would receive from them was that my product was bulky. I would then leverage a success story to help ease this concern. It usually went something like this: "You are not the first to tell me that my product feels bulky. When I was training at a large health system like yours, I frequently heard that this product was bulky. However, after six months of using the product, those same nurses came through the refresher training and told me how the shape was actually helpful for them because they were able to place it down easier and take care of their patients."

Not every story is going to resonate with every person. Be intentional about listening to stories from your customers that can help you tell of the success of your product in a way that captures your customers' attention.

Testimonials

I can pretty much guarantee you leverage testimonials all the time personally, so why would you not use it to sell your idea?! Think about it: When you are purchasing something online, you look at the star rating (testimonial). When you read the customer reviews before buying (testimonial). When you ask a friend about a good restaurant to try (testimonial).

To *love* sales, you need to get your current customers to share their positive experiences working with you and using what you sell with your prospective customers. There are many resources on ways to share testimonials, but consider how you could leverage print, videos, calls, blogs, online forums, etc., to get the word out.

A personal testimonial example for me was when I went to buy an offset meat smoker. I read reviews online and looked in hardware stores. I asked each of my friends who had different types of smokers their opinion. What did they like or not like about what they were using? What did they wish they had?

The best testimonial came from a co-worker who had almost 6–7 different types of grills in his backyard. He was a "master" when it came to cooking any type of meat in any way. I was vacillating between a pellet smoker and a charcoal smoker. Both had advantages and disadvantages. However, when my co-worker said to me, "Charcoal offset smokers are messy, but the food sure does taste the best," I had made my decision.

I am 100% satisfied with my charcoal offset smoker purchase. I'm not here to get into an argument, and I'm sure I've lost a few of you because you use an electric, drum, or pellet smoker, and that is okay. The important thing to re-member is that you probably already read or give testimonials naturally in your personal life but are afraid to ask your customers in business to support you.

Hint: if you cannot ask your customers to help you, you need to go back and ask better open-ended questions, provide more value, and be more intention-al in connecting emotionally because you do not have as great of a relation-ship with that customer as you may think.

Best Practices

If you knew something that someone else could use to perform better, would you share it? I would hope so! In sales, you will get to meet many different types of people. You will see many different types of businesses and how they are run (some good and some not-so-good). You will see services that attract lots of clients. You will see technical experts in their industry who sur-pass their peers.

Be a ravenous notetaker on each of these things! To *love* sales, you must be hyper-observant so that you can find the value you can deliver to others. If you bring value to others, you will improve their world in some way, and that, hopefully, will have a positive emotional impact on them.

When I called on office managers who ran outpatient medical practices, I would often get questions from them on how to best advertise their practice. These decision-makers were tasked with getting more patients in the door (need) and were curious how other practices were attracting patients (value).

Since I kept hearing this common need across all my customers, I started to be diligent when I approached a practice to see how they were advertising. I would look them up online and see how their online presence looked. I would watch the staff interactions with patients to see their level of friendliness. I would look around the waiting room to see what types of content were out on the tables or screens.

Since I could see anywhere from 5–8 customers in a day, over the course of a few months, I started to gain a lot of insights into those practices that were busy and doing well, and those that could use a little help. I would keep notes, and then as I met with office managers who were curious about advertising, I would share the various ideas and best practices I had seen from other practices to bring value.

I could then go a step further and offer to help "kick-start" some of the advertising I was recommending based on the programs I was able to sell. Even if I didn't have immediate business, collaborating on an advertising program with the office manager could establish a partnership with the account over time. Sharing best practices was a way for me to build a trusting relationship with my customer and provide a high level of value.

To *love* sales, you must remain vigilant and watch for ways to bring value to your customers during every part of your day—even when waiting.

POSITIVE ASSOCIATIONS

When my son turned ten, the energy drink PRIME was all the rage. He wanted it at his birthday party and all his friends wanted it too. Everyone thought his party was "so cool" because everyone had a PRIME to drink.

For my son, there was a positive association between PRIME being "athletic" and "cool," which he *really* needed as a ten-year-old. Funny how all his friends had the same positive association. Not one of his friends looked at the PRIME drink and said, "Naw, I don't want it. I'm not a fan." Each one embraced PRIME with exuberance.

To *love* sales, you want your customers to positively associate with you and what you are selling. Have you spent time thinking about the type of emotions your customers have when they interact with you or your product/service? When you share your idea, have you thought about how it may be perceived? What positive emotional associations do you have with a product like my son did with PRIME?

I had a small office customer who would spend hours on the phone trying to verify insurance coverage for her patients. Sometimes, she would wait on hold for 60 minutes for the insurance company to answer, and then they would not be able to give her what she needed. She was spending hours and hours online and on the phone verifying benefits.

One of the services I sold had a 24–48-hour turnaround on verification of insurance coverage after uploading a short 5–10-minute request form. After that request form was submitted, the next response from the service would be the verified insurance coverage. She would no longer need to wait 60 minutes on hold or submit requests between patients.

Every time I checked in with the customer, there was a positive association between me and my service because of the amount of time I saved her. I provided value with my service, but I helped her emotionally feel much more productive since she was not on the phone for hours. Remember to pay particular attention to improvements in time, effort, or ease of use and the potential problem your product/service solves for the customer to understand the emotions of why people buy.

Creating an Emotional Connection with a Customer

Who is someone you have a strong emotional connection with? It may be a parent, spouse, friend, or roommate. How did you build that emotional connection? Did it just automatically happen? Of course not! You took time to build and cultivate that relationship so that it was meaningful to both of you.

I remember when my wife and I were dating. I did everything I could to build an emotional connection with her. I wrote her personalized cards and asked her out. We went on dates together where we spent time talking about our hobbies, passions, history, goals, ambitions, childhood, and more. During each of these interactions, we were building emotional connections and learning if this person was "the one" we wanted to spend the rest of our lives with!

Now, I'm not saying that you need to "date" your customers, but when you think about how you can build an emotional connection, it is helpful to think about how you do it personally to see what is transferrable to the business world. I'm not in any way condoning participating in any illicit or shady behavior with your customer to get a sale. Nor am I saying that you should physically *love* your customer.

Let's look at a few examples of how to *love* sales by building emotional connections with customers so they feel valued, understood, and want to buy!

PERSONALIZATION

When you get a handwritten thank you note, how does it start? "Dear [insert name], thank you for the..." That note is addressed specifically to you, with the writer telling you exactly what they are thankful for that you gave them. Meanwhile, I have gotten plenty of "thank you" notes from retailers after I have made a purchase with them, usually with a discount code, so that I can come back and purchase again real soon. I am much more interested in a personalized note and more likely to have an emotional response to a personalized note without strings attached.

To get to know your customers better and to help make your interactions more personalized, I would recommend using the Mackay 66 Customer Profile tool

(Harvey Mackay Academy, n.d.). This profile captures information on who the customer is, their educational background, family information, their business background, special interests, and lifestyle. While this level of detail may seem unnecessary for a customer, think back to my example about my wife.

Learning more about someone helps to create a deeper relationship—and, therefore, a deeper emotional connection.

Being able to intentionally follow up based on what you learned about them previously shows interest versus only being focused on "closing the sale."

As we discussed during the open-ended questions section, a key part of asking questions is listening to the answers. You should train your ear to listen to those items mentioned above as some of them come out in normal conversation. You don't need to interrogate your customers to be able to complete the whole list. (I hope you wouldn't do that on a first date, or you may not get a second!)

For example, the customer may tell you that they just took their child on a college visit to ABC College, and they are going to have to make a decision soon on where to go. Wow, this is a lot of good information. You now know:

1. They have a child who is probably a junior or senior in high school.
2. They are interested in higher education.
3. They gave you the name of the college or university they are interested in.
4. They shared the emotional stressors they may be going through over the next few months as they complete the paperwork and decision process.

Remaining emotionally aware, this may be a great time to ask follow-up questions to get to know your customer better, too. You could ask them:

1. about their schooling experience
2. how they decided which college to attend
3. what are their thoughts on the decision process
4. how they feel about their child going off to school
5. what major(s), sport(s), or societies they were a part of in school.

You are being curious, building a relationship, and focusing on the best interest of the customer. As you make your sales calls over the next few months, you can follow up on their child's college acceptance journey. This is applicable to many situations, including buying a car, a house, having a child, getting married, children getting married, where they are going on vacation, favorite sports teams, previous roles, community activities, etc.

One of the best salespeople I have ever worked with was a master at this. Whenever he walked into a customer's office, he would know the receptionist's name and what was going on with her that weekend; he would ask detailed and relevant questions so there was evidence of a true emotional connection.

What made him a master was he didn't just do this with the receptionist; he had relationships with every level, from c-suite to janitor. He knew them by name and what was going on in their life. He took detailed notes and practiced remembering this information to personalize his approach with them later. He made sure that every person in the office felt special through an emotional connection to him and therefore created a better chance of him closing a sale. By the way, he *loves* sales!

FOLLOW-UP AND CARE

There is a common misperception that the sale is over once a purchase order is received—wrong! This viewpoint is self-focused, not customer-focused. You, as the salesperson, have spent weeks, months, maybe years working to get that PO, so it is quite an accomplishment! However, the customer just *started* their relationship with you when they signed the PO.

Let's go back to our dating example. You wouldn't work for weeks or months to ask out that special someone only to not show up on the date! You worked hard to get them to commit to going out with you, and they now said yes! Naturally, you would show up because you're excited to go out with them.

When you *love* sales, you realize that the customer is most important, and when they say "yes," it is just the beginning of the sales process, not the end. Think of everything you can accomplish now that you have full access to the account because your customer is now using your product or service:

- You can be present more often and see other potential areas for improvement.
- You can meet more people because you need to train or to follow up on usage.
- You can ask follow-up questions to make sure your product or service is as effective as you said it would be.

Remember, your customer just bought from you and is ready to begin a long-term relationship. How you follow up, ask for feedback, and support the customer will be critical to whether the relationship survives long-term.

When I was selling a hand-held medical device, I closed a six-hospital sale for over $1,000,000. That was a good personal payday for me. However, the customer was just getting started with the product, and I needed to be sure they were happy and understood how to use it effectively.

To make sure I was intentional about following up with my new customer, I created a schedule where I visited each hospital on a regular basis and met with a variety of departments to make sure everything was working properly. I took the good feedback and shared it with my leadership team. I took the bad feedback and shared it with my leadership team.

Having a large customer who was willing to provide feedback, both positive and negative, helped me understand potential benefits and pain points with future customers. This insight enabled me to identify these aspects during my questioning and selling process. Best of all, my customer knew that I would be there for them to find an answer to every question they raised.

EMPATHETIC PROBLEM-SOLVING

There are going to be problems with your product or service. Nothing works 100% of the time, whether it is a physical item or a service being provided. If you are ready to help your customer through the challenges and anticipate them, you will be ahead of the curve. If you haven't yet encountered the issue, work with your customer to have them help you come up with solutions when applicable.

When I sold a point of care device, the device would take the sample in a horizontal position, and then the user would tip the device straight up vertically, causing the sample to drain down into the sensor, resulting in issues. I knew this was a problem, so during my selling process and customer training, I would work to mitigate the potential issue by helping the customer follow the steps to make the process the most enjoyable.

Did the product still need to be cleaned? Yes. Did some staff members still repeatedly use it incorrectly? Yes. However, I worked with them to understand the problem (in this case, it was a habit from previous devices) so that I could understand what it was like to be in their shoes.

If you sell something and then never come back to check on the customer and see how they are using it, you'll never know if your product is working the way you expect.

If you really like someone on your first few dates and then have one fight and never talk with them again, you could be missing out. Being willing to be empathetic and trying to understand the other person's point of view (either your date or customer) will help you approach problem-solving differently.

To *love* sales, think of obstacles and problems as a challenge to work through together that will help you bond with your customer—not an annoyance to ignore.

SURPRISE AND DELIGHT

My family and I love to go to the Deerfield Fair in New Hampshire. We have a great time seeing the animals, eating too much fair food, and visiting the various barns showcasing products/services/crafts. One particular year, we had purchased tickets in advance and printed them out but forgot to bring them with us. (Hey, it happens to the best of us.)

Now, one nice thing about the fair is that it is out in the country, but the downside about the country is that cell coverage is not usually stellar. So, we didn't have our tickets, and our phone wouldn't download the tickets because there was no cell coverage. We had purchased them, but we couldn't show proof.

As we approached the gate, we met a nice older gentleman who was scanning everyone's tickets. We told him our story, and he looked at us for a brief second and then said, "Bloop, bloop," as he fake-scanned our nonexistent tickets and allowed us into the fair. We were surprised and overjoyed!

That gentleman could have said, "Sorry, you must show your ticket, or you cannot enter. Go to the kiosk behind you and purchase new tickets." His generosity made our day when he could have made it quite difficult.

Be mindful of ways in which you can surprise and delight your customers:

- Can you auto-enroll them in a loyalty program for discounts?
- Can you celebrate them through a customer appreciation event?
- Can you remember their birthday or anniversary with a card or coffee?
- Can you give them a free upgrade due to their loyalty to get their feedback?
- Can you give them exclusive access before others?
- Can you add a personalized note or video expressing your gratitude for them?

Tap into your creativity and let the ideas flow. Your surprise or delight does not have to be big or expensive. However, it does need to be thoughtful, intentional, and focused on the customer. If you are going to surprise your significant other with flowers or chocolate, make sure they are the colors and type of chocolate she likes, not just "flowers" or your favorite chocolate.

I had a loyal account that would not let many salespeople into their office. I was one of just two that was welcomed behind the front desk. Every now and then, I would bring with me some sample product to leave with the account. Due to company and industry restrictions, I only had a certain quota of samples I could leave with any customer each year. Therefore, receiving sample products was a real treat.

I loved surprising my customers because each time I brought in those samples, the joy on their faces and how it would impact their office and patients would shine through. Plus, it was always fun to hear the stories during follow-up visits of those patients who had been able to use those samples and the impact they had on many lives.

To *love* sales, be mindful, have fun, and enjoy the smile you bring to your customer when you exceed their expectations with a surprise gift, discount, or other delight.

The E in the LOVE Sales Framework™ builds upon how each of us are emotional beings and in need of emotional connection to move forward in the buying process. We have explored how we can understand ourselves through emotional intelligence, building trust, understanding empathy, and understanding emotions for buying with customers. Thinking of your customer more than yourself will help you be intentional in your interactions during the ups and downs of the selling process.

I hope you *love* the emotional connections you make with your customers through the LOVE Sales Framework™!

Questions to Consider

1. Which area of emotional intelligence is most difficult for you (Self-awareness, Self-regulation, or Empathy)? How can you work to improve that area?

2. How do you build rapport or trust with others? When did it go well? When was it a challenge?

3. Who have you had empathy for? How did it feel?

4.   How can you practice having empathy for others?

5.   How natural does it feel for you to have empathy for others?

6.   How are you responsible, clear, and authentic with your customers and friends?

7. What was a purchase you made using emotion? How did it turn out for you? Why?

8. When did someone personalize their interaction with you? How did it make you feel?

9. What is something you have a positive association with? Why? How did it start or grow?

10. When was the last time you were surprised or delighted? What happened? Why was it a surprise or delight?

6

Decoding LOVE: Recognizing its Forms and Distortions

There is a big difference between knowing and doing. You can know all about something, but you must do something to fully understand it.

After one of my training sessions on asking questions, I met a retired National Football League (NFL) player who was just starting his career in sales. As a high performer, he fell in love with sales due to its quick pace, competitive nature, and rewards system. He approached me and asked, "how can I become a master at asking questions like you?" I asked him, "did you immediately start playing football in the NFL?" He laughed and said, "of course not!"

That was exactly the point. We discussed how he started in peewee football at a young age to begin learning the fundamentals of the game. As he progressed through middle-and high-school he learned more complicated offensive and defensive plays. When he went to college he learned a new playbook with more advanced players, workouts, and games. Finally, when he joined the NFL, he continued to improve his game and learned even more tactical applications. The fundamental rules of American Football are essentially the same at all levels of the game; however, the complexity of the playbook and the caliber of the players increases at each level of play.

"This is going to take time," he said. He is exactly right. In football, he knew the right moves, formations, and tactics and practiced how to perfect and recognize each of them. The same is true in sales. It is going to take time to get fluent with learning how to set goals, ask questions, determine what is valuable to the customer, and understand the emotions of why they buy.

This is the importance of the LOVE Sales Framework™. It is designed to lay the foundation for you to *love* sales and perform at the highest level. This is going to take time and work. You will need to practice, get out of your comfort zone, and be intentional. Each area of the framework can help you succeed if you *act* upon it—not just know it.

Whatever your overall ambition is in sales, in the next few chapters, we will focus on the different types of *love*, what love does not look like, how you can integrate the LOVE Sales Framework™ into your sales process, improve your mindset, become more resilient, and build your confidence. Let's start with an important question about love.

Different Types of LOVE

What do you think of when you think of the word love? Do you think of a person or action? What about the phrase, "I love you." Does that evoke feelings of happiness and positive emotions or challenges and anxious emotions from previous hurts? When do you find yourself saying you genuinely "*love*" something or someone? Or is the word *love* just part of your daily vernacular?

In working with one of my team members, she would frequently use the word love in her writing. "I *love* that idea," or, "I *love* that you said ..." When we chatted about her writings together, she would acknowledge that she regularly overused the word love. She challenged herself to be more precise and to re-think how and when she used the word.

If you flippantly use the word *love*, do you actually know what it means? A better question is, do you think *love* actually has a place in the business world? Is it inappropriate to say *love* in the workplace? Or to others?

---

*My challenge to you is that, yes, **love** belongs in the workplace, but not in the way you may think.*

According to C.S. Lewis in his book *The Four Loves*, there are four different types of *love*: Affection, Friendship, Eros, and Charity. Let's consider each of them briefly below.

AFFECTION (FAMILIAL, STORGE LOVE)

This type of *love* is one that is characterized by one that you might find in a family or empathy bond. It is a natural, instinctive *love*, one that exists within families or close relationships (like between a parent and a child). A few characteristics include:

Familiarity: This is the shared experiences of daily interactions together. Strong familial bonds are built by spending time together and becoming emotionally close through shared experiences.

Warmth: This *love* makes you feel "at home" or secure within the family unit. Visiting a grandparent's house or childhood home can evoke comforting feelings reflecting the warmth of this type of *love*.

Acceptance: This type of *love* is one that accepts one another—flaws and all. None of us are perfect. We all have flaws. True acceptance love acknowledges and embraces the uniqueness of each family member no matter their flaws or situation.

Unconditional: This *love* is a steadfast and enduring *love* that persists even in challenging times. No matter the situation, how much time passes, or our various surroundings, families *love* each other through all of it. There will be moments everyone does not "like" each other, but they will always *love* each other.

Protective Instinct: This *love* helps us be protective of each other. Rarely does a family member watch another family member intentionally run toward danger. We want to look out for the well-being and safety of all family members.

FRIENDSHIP (PHILIA LOVE)

While storge *love* refers mainly to family, philia *love* focuses on friendship or deep companionship. You may have heard this type of love called brotherly love, too. You could consider this type of love of shared understanding, shared values, or strong bonds between individuals. This type of love goes beyond casual friendship and represents a deeper, intentional, and reciprocal connection. A few characteristics include:

Mutual Respect: To *love* sales, you must realize you are going to be selling to another person and you should celebrate the uniqueness of that person. Your customer will have a different perspective, opinion, or lifestyle, but you must work to embrace those differences to appreciate the diversity that each person brings to the friendship.

Shared Interests: To *love* sales, you need to find areas where you share common interests with your customers by asking good questions and listening to them. To find common interests, you need to know a lot about a little to learn your shared interests.

Reciprocity: To *love* sales, you need to not just talk about yourself. There must be two-way communication where each person is investing and engaged in the relationship to build a long-term connection. Note: reciprocity takes time and effort so be gracious, curious, and open to learning new things to connect better with others.

Trust: To *love* sales and be successful, it is important to respect your customers' information and do not break their trust. As A.D. Ryan says, "Trust takes years to build, seconds to break and forever to repair" ("A Quote from Just a Number" n.d.).

Your legacy and how you present yourself with others, and how you treat others, will be what is most remembered by your customers.

Intellectual Connection: To *love* sales, you must be able to engage in meaningful conversations, discussions, and be able to share thoughts and ideas that build connections. You may never be as knowledgeable about a certain topic as some of your customers, but you can learn about a topic to carry on a stimulating conversation for both of you, which will lead to more trust, mutual respect, and reciprocity.

Endurance: To *love* sales, you must have personal endurance to overcome the daily setbacks, as you work with customers to understand them and their timeframes. This means showing up the same yesterday, today, and tomorrow knowing that you may not get a sale for months, or even years, but you believe in your product or service enough that you are willing to keep going and trying to build the friendships to provide long-term customer value.

As you implement the LOVE Sales Framework™, remember that Philia will be the predominant type of love that you will use when connecting with customers. Not every customer will be your best friend, but over time you can build respect, intellectual connection, shared interests, trust, and reciprocity throughout your sales journey.

EROS LOVE

When the word *love* is mentioned, most people probably think of eros, or romantic/passionate *love*. It is all around us, highlighted in commercials, movies, TV shows, billboards, songs, books, and more. It focuses on desire, attraction, and commitment.

Eros *love* is an important *love* between two people, but it does not fit into the

LOVE Sales Framework™. Having an amorous or illicit relationship with your customer to get a sale or because you think it will fast-track you to success is wrong. I have not heard of a successful sales consultant who leveraged eros *love* with their customer to achieve a long-term, lasting customer relationship. Avoid eros *love* in your business relationships—it will not end well.

AGAPE (DIVINE LOVE)

C.S. Lewis regarded agape *love* as the highest and purist form of *love*. It is a selfless, sacrificial, and unconditional *love* that goes beyond personal feelings or attractions. As a Christian, agape *love* is best demonstrated through Jesus Christ.

> John 3:16 (NIV) says, *"For God so loved the world that he gave his one and only Son, that whoever believes in him shall not perish but have eternal life."*

> Romans 8:39 (NIV) says, *"Neither height nor depth, nor anything else in all creation, will be able to separate us from the love of God that is in Christ Jesus our Lord."*

Christians believe that everyone is sinful (aka immoral) and cannot stand in front of a holy God because sin has separated them from God. So, God sent his Son, Jesus Christ, who never sinned, to be a perfect sacrifice for sin by dying on a cross, rising from the dead three days later, and creating a way for you to be able to be accepted as pure before a holy God.

This type of *love* is incomprehensible for us. I do not pretend to understand the full depths of how agape *love* works. Let's explore a few areas about agape *love*:

Selfless: "You gotta look out for #1!" Selfless *love* is a truly complete lack of self-interest. For all of us on earth, this is impossible, but it is not for God (hence, the divine *love*). This *love* focuses on the well-being of others without any type of reciprocity. No acknowledgement or benefit, just pure, selflessness focused on others. While you cannot embody this 100%, how can you think less of yourself and more of your customer?

Sacrifice: As we think of this in the context of divine *love*, Jesus sacrificed his entire life for the sins of the world. He sacrificed His own needs, desire, and well-being for the sake of others. Sacrifice requires actions for the benefit of others. While we all make sacrifices, how much of the sacrifice is for your own personal gain? Do you diet to look good, or work out to feel good, or make sales only for the money? How can you think more of sacrificial *love* for others?

Unconditional: This has been mentioned before, but in the context of agape *love*, this is independent of the worthiness of who is receiving it. In storge *love*, the family unit loves because that person is part of the family. With agape *love*, the *love* is extended freely, without reservation, for anyone at any time. This embodies a concept called grace. When a Christian accepts Christ as their Savior through grace, there are no conditions upon that acceptance. Immediately upon acceptance, they are saved from their sins. There is no need to "get right" or "figure it out" or "clean up my life" before acceptance. Those would be conditions, and agape *love* is unconditional for anyone. How can you think about everyone in the sales process as having value?

Universal: Agape *love* extends to all humanity. It is universal, not just one focused on personal relationships, friendships or family. Agape *love* does not demarcate on age, sex, occupation, location, education, etc. You could be the wealthiest person in the world, or barely making it, and agape *love* applies to you. While we continually work to remove our inherent bias towards others, agape *love* has no bias and extends to all. During your sales process, how can you look beyond a bias of a person or account and approach the customer with *love*?

I recognize this section on agape *love* may be uncomfortable for you. You may have had a bad experience in a church growing up, or you may have certain beliefs that counter with what I just described.

Ultimately, the importance of discussing the different types of *love* is to help you become a sales consultant with your customers that focuses less on what you will gain, and more on what your customer can gain. In almost all the loves described above (storge, philia, agape), the reciprocity and mutual benefit of the relationship is what is critical. When thinking about the LOVE Sales Framework™, it's important to consider how you can integrate *love* into your sales process.

What LOVE Does NOT Look Like

To try to see all viewpoints, I enjoy taking the "devil's advocate" position when it comes to various topics. The premise is to think of the opposite of what you are working on and to see if you have thought of all the different approaches that should be considered.

We have talked a lot about what it looks like to *love* sales, but what does it look like to NOT *love* sales? Sure, you could try to take each of the areas in the LOVE Sales Framework™ and think of the opposite thing to do, but it is not quite that simple. I challenge you to think of a personal example of when you did not show or receive *love*, and you can begin to realize that *love* goes much deeper.

In talking with another sales consultant, she told me a story about when she traveled out in the field for the first time. She was from a big city and was asked to go on a field ride. She had to fly to a very off-the-grid location and coordinate her own way from the airport to the hotel. The sales consultant she was shadowing had told her he would pick her up in the morning.

She gets a call in the morning saying that he was not going to be able to pick her up, and he wanted her to meet him at the first account, two hours away. Yikes, not a warm, friendly welcome. When they officially met, he did not ask her any questions or help guide her in sales. He made her follow him in her car to each of their meetings. During lunch, they stopped at a gas station, and he said he was just going to eat in his own car by himself, so she had to eat on her own. Finally, at the end of the day, when he was close to his house, he said they were done, and she now had a three-hour drive back to her hotel.

Did that sales consultant officially do anything wrong? Probably not. He met with her, they went to accounts, and then they parted ways. However, his actions during the day demonstrated that he did not want to be with her. He made her go out of her way to meet him, stayed separate when there was a time for connection and mentorship over lunch, and didn't care that he missed an opportunity to guide and coach a younger sales consultant on how to be successful.

Most of your customers will be able to tell if you really want to connect with them or if you are just going through the motions.

Let's look at a few examples of how NOT to show *love* in the sales process.

TRICK THE CUSTOMER

We have all worked with that shady sales consultant who will say anything to get the deal. They will tell you it's the end of the month and they are going to offer you a deal. Or that they were able to get special pricing for you. Unfortunately, trickery seems to be more common in the car sales business. I'm not saying all car salespeople are shady, but it can feel like they are trying to trick their buyers.

When I was in the market for a new car, I was comparing lots of different models. I had found a used car I liked at a small used car dealership just about 20 minutes away from my house. I drove out and took the car on a test drive. The salesman insisted on going with me and said that we only had 30 minutes because he then had to leave to have a dialysis treatment for his kidney issues.

I told him I would not make a purchase of a car without my wife seeing it, so we agreed to meet halfway so that she could see the car, too. While my wife was there, I realized we were past his time to head to his dialysis appointment. I quickly approached and said we should head back so he could get to his appointment, but he told me it was okay, and we still had time.

My wife and I parted ways, and I had to drive the salesman back to the dealership. Along the way, he continued to tell me all the great features of this car and why I should drive away in it today. I was already feeling a little strange that he was late for his dialysis appointment, but I listened to him talk about his family, the car features, and how long he had been in sales. When we got back to the car dealer's office, which was long after he needed to leave for his appointment, he told me it was okay that he was missing his appointment and he could reschedule.

He then proceeded to tell me that he was going to give me a deal for that day only and that I would have to sign within the next hour, or it would expire. He was going to make sure he got me the best price he could by calling his management team so I could walk out with that car that instant. However, when I asked him if he had the title in hand so that if I paid cash, I could walk away with ownership on that day, he could not tell me where the title was. He kept telling me, "We have it, don't worry." Yeah, that made me feel *really* confident. I thanked the man, wished him the best with his appointment, which was now long gone, and never had any intention of calling or working with that dealership again.

Why go into so much detail here? Because while the salesman was trying to make me feel important and that I was his top priority, he ultimately wanted me to buy that car on that day because that benefited him. He didn't need or care about the title because once he got paid, someone else had to work those details out, and it wouldn't be him.

He would be off on the next test ride, playing to the emotions of his clients on how he was fighting a bad disease. While the disease part may be true, telling a brand-new potential client within the first 30 minutes that you had a disease did not help build rapport or trust with me. Ultimately, his tactics were to trick or pressure me into a sale that I was not comfortable making. I can imagine he has worked with others who were very emotionally connected to his stories and felt the pressure to make a decision that they may have regretted.

If you don't *love* sales, you think only of your own personal gain and try to trick, bribe, or pressure the customer into an action that benefits you, not them. Put the customer first, and they will become a customer for life instead of a single transaction.

YOU ARE WRONG

Lots of sales books will tell you that the customer is always right. No, the customer is not always right, but that doesn't mean that you point out their flaws. The customer is who is going to buy your product, so you must learn to understand what they are thinking. If you tell them they are wrong, you are telling them that their emotions or thoughts are not validated.

Customers get wrong ideas or perceptions based on a variety of factors. If you begin arguing with your customer about who is right, the customer is even more likely to dig their heels in and not move forward with you. However, if you can politely ask for additional clarity using great open-ended questions, you can help your customer understand where their knowledge gap may be and bridge it rather than challenge it.

Let's have a reality check here—this is hard. Some people are more naturally confrontational than others. However, all of us, at some point, have been wrong. We may have intentionally kept our wrong thinking only to spite the other person from having the satisfaction of telling them they were right. Or, because of what we were told or heard, we may not even know we were wrong.

I love the confidence of young children. One day after school, my 8-year-old son came home and told me, "Daddy, my friend told me the biggest number in school today." As any good parent, I was thinking, "How fun, he learned about infinity today." He then proceeded to tell me, "The number is Google." Being his dad, I, of course, said, "Oh really? I thought the largest number was infinity." His response was, "You're wrong, Dad; Google is the biggest number. Infinity is just a sideways eight."

Now, I had a decision to make. My son was young, and I knew he was wrong. Should I berate him and tell him how dumb he is to think that Google is the largest number? Could I use the situation as a learning opportunity? Could I just drop the whole thing and realize he will probably forget about it over the next five minutes as he moves on to his next task? He was given the wrong information, and he believed it. It was going to take time to change his mind since he was told by a credible source (his friend) and at a credible place (school).

Remember, your customer is going to have the wrong information. It's only human to have wrong information. A sales professional who does NOT *love* the customer will argue and challenge them at the expense of a long-term relationship. Remember our discussion on philia love. As you build emotional connections (the E in the LOVE Sales Framework™), you will be leveraging philia love with concepts of mutual respect, reciprocity, and intellectual connection. Before you decide to engage in an argument and tell your customer they are wrong, think about if you are being clear, responsible, authentic, and communicative with the customer in that moment. If not, that argument will likely not result in building trust but will lead to more distrust of you, your company, and your product or service.

There may be times when you must address your customers because they are wrong. Each of these situations must be approached collaboratively and as a partnership.

Your goal should be to help the customer make an informed decision, not to show them you are right.

Below is a brief list of areas where you may need to confront:

- Clarifying Misunderstandings: If your customer has misunderstood how a particular product or an aspect of your service works, you should gently challenge their perspective to ensure clarity.
- Addressing Concerns: If the customer has incorrect information, you should work to help them have accurate facts about your product, service, or idea but do so in a diplomatic manner.

- Presenting Alternatives: If you have done a good job with the O in the LOVE Sales Framework™, you have asked a lot of open-ended questions and have a good understanding of the customer's goals and objectives. If the customer is moving in a direction away from these stated goals, you can gently challenge them to make sure you fully understand their goals to try to get them back on track. Work to focus on guidance versus disagreement.

- Encouraging Strategic Thinking: If you are helping the customer to think differently, you are doing a great job as a sales consultant. However, sometimes customers get short-sighted and need a consultant to help them challenge the short-term outcome compared to long-term benefits. Help your customer to see how you are helping them reach their long-term goals.

WASTE THEIR TIME

During my annual physical, my doctor asked me to book an appointment with another department of the hospital. She said they could do a telehealth appointment with me so it would be quick and could be scheduled soon. I thanked her and waited for their call.

About a week later, I received a phone call from that department. The lady on the phone was pleasant and asked what date would work well for me. I told her I wanted to do a telehealth appointment. She informed me that they do not do telehealth appointments. Then she asked me what day would work for me to come into the office. I suggested a Monday or a Friday. She then said those were the surgeon's operating days, and no appointments were available.

Next, she asked me what month would be good to book and gave me an option of six months in the future—so much for a timely appointment. She asked if I wanted a morning or afternoon. I said a morning would be good, and she told me the options six months out were booked and proceeded to ask if an appointment eight months out would work for me. I said yes, hung up the phone, and was completely frustrated!

She was very pleasant. She asked me good, relevant questions to try to meet my needs. She had my needs in mind by asking what would work best for me. Ultimately, she wasted my time. I did not have a timely appointment. I could not do a telehealth appointment. I could not get an appointment on a Monday or Friday. I could not come in sooner than six months. I could not get a morning appointment for another two months. If this receptionist does not have the ability to affect the outcome, do not make her ask so many questions. Those questions just irritated me and made me want to cancel the appointment altogether. Since it is for my health, I felt obligated to keep the appointment, but I will be looking for a new medical provider.

You can still have the best intentions to focus on the customer and ask relevant questions, but if you cannot meet their goals or have too much "red tape" to sift through, you do not show much *love* for your customer.

The key point here is to make sure you do not waste your customers' time. Their time, and yours, is precious, and if you are getting some of it, treat it with the respect and honor it deserves.

REMEMBER:
1. Your customer does not have to meet with you.
2. Your customer does not have to listen to you.
3. Your customer does not have to care about you.
4. Your customer DOES have to stay in business.
5. Your customer DOES have to service their clients.
6. Your customer DOES have to get work done, too (and is looking for ways to do it faster, better, and cheaper).

DIARRHEA OF THE MOUTH

This was often a term that my father used after a salesperson had come to his office and just talked through the majority of the meeting—not transferring value or creating a dialogue, but just talking about products, services, or anything else under the sun. Too much talking because of nerves or blank space in a conversation will make you hate sales. You may be an introvert, so talking feels unnatural, and then you keep talking to fill the space, which feels even more unnatural, and then you don't feel confident at the end of the call because all you did was talk.

Let's think about the impact this will have on your customer.

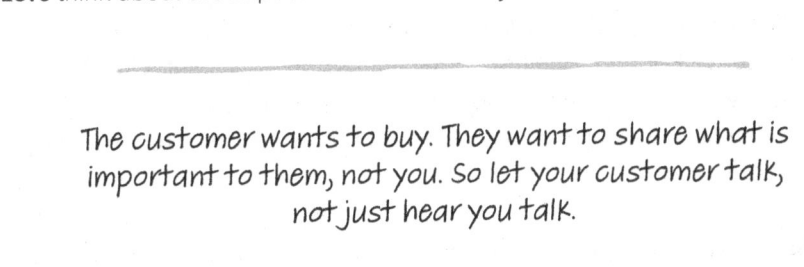

The customer wants to buy. They want to share what is important to them, not you. So let your customer talk, not just hear you talk.

You might think this is offensive, and you would be justified in that comment, but it's unpleasant on purpose. This type of language is a reminder of how it feels to just be talked at versus carrying on a conversation.

One of my favorite activities during sales trainings is the selling scenarios. The consultants are eager to practice what they have learned and to share all the facts they memorized. Inevitably, during each selling scenario, the sales consultant will ask a closed-ended question, the customer will respond quickly, and then the sales consultant lists every single fact about the product. Since it is sales training, the customer is sympathetic and listens to the full answer, but the long-winded, fact-based, pontification does not help the sales consultant move the sales process forward or build any connection with the customer. The feedback from the trainers is to get the customer talking and ask them what they think versus just spouting facts excessively. Too many sales consultants just talk to fill blank space.

Proverbs 17:27 (CSB) says, *"The one who has knowledge restrains his words, and one who keeps a cool head is a person of understanding."*

When you're tempted to have diarrhea of the mouth with your customer because you are nervous, unsure, uncomfortable, or for any other reason—STOP! Reframe what you want to hear from your customer and have them tell you what is ailing them rather than you diagnosing them yourself. If you let the customer tell you their problems, you will *love* the sales you start to make by listening to them versus talking too much. Don't make the customer sick with your diarrhea of the mouth.

LIE TO THE CUSTOMER

What will you say to get a sale? Will you compromise your integrity? Your word? Your company? Lying can destroy a relationship in an instant. One moment you have credibility, the next moment you can be deemed untrustworthy. One moment you have a positive impression on people and the next moment your name is tarnished.

LIE: I'm late to this appointment because there was a car accident on my way over.

TRUTH: I didn't get up in time to make it to this appointment on time. I'll make sure to set my alarm earlier next time.

LIE: My product is on backorder so it's not available today.

TRUTH: I forgot to bring my product with me today, so it's not available. I'll make sure to have it for you tomorrow.

LIE: We can totally provide that many sessions to you and have done so with other customers.

TRUTH: This request is something beyond what we have committed to before, let's chat more to make sure we can truly service your needs.

If you choose to lie about your product, skills, company, or anything else, be prepared to *hate* sales in the long-term. Yes, you may *love* the short-term gains lying can win for you in sales, but your reputation will be tarnished. Ultimately, your shady ways will be uncovered. You may become known as the sales consultant who exaggerates claims, conceals information, or even gives false promises.

I am often reminded of the phrase, "You only get one chance to make a first impression." Embrace each of your sales interactions as a first impression and you will be hyper-vigilant to remain customer focused. Remember, your customer may have worked with a previous sales consultant that lied to them and overpromised-underdelivered. It is going to take time for them to trust you since lying destroys trust.

> Proverbs 26:28 (CSB) says, *"A lying tongue hates those it crushes, and a flattering mouth causes ruin."*

> Proverbs 12:19 (ESV) says, *"Truthful lips endure forever, but a lying tongue is but for a moment."*

> Matthew 5:37a (CSB) says, *"But let your 'yes' mean 'yes,' and your 'no' mean 'no.'"*

These verses remind us of the importance of our words. They can crush those we interact with, ruin relationships, and cause fleeting success. When you tell the truth, you are working towards long-term, sustainable relationships. As the old saying goes, "Say what you mean and mean what you say."

I'm reminded of what my parents told me in Chapter 3 when we were discussing establishing trust: "If you tell the truth, you never have to remember what you said." The same is true here when it comes to lying. If you tell the truth, you do not have to remember the lies you tell your customers. If you tell the truth, you will build more meaningful, long-term emotional connections because you will be responsible, clear, authentic and seen as ethical in your interactions.

To *love* sales, you must always tell the truth. This will be hard. Very hard. But to *love* sales long-term, your success, and reputation, depends on the words that come out of your mouth. The adage "Honesty is the best policy," has stood the test of time because it is *correct!* Honesty is *always* the best policy.

Lying may feel completely natural to you. It may be something that you have justified due to circumstances, relationships, protection, or any other number of reasons. My challenge to you is to stop this behavior. It will be hard, but as you study your triggers, environment, and motives, you can understand and practice how honesty really is the best policy.

Some may even say that lying in sales has become acceptable because of its permeability within the profession. Exaggerating product features, a "white lie" here or there, omitting key information, or just not telling the truth seems commonplace nowadays. You may have had a mentor, trainer, or peer even guide you to lie to your customer. Remember, a lie is a lie—plain and simple. If you choose to lie, you will eventually *hate* sales.

To *love* sales, be known as a consultant of integrity and always tell the truth.

In this chapter, we looked at the different types of love and embraced a devil's advocate position on how NOT to show love in the sales process. Now, you may be thinking, "I need to do these things to get the sale!" Wrong. Lying, tricking, dawdling, arguing, or pontificating with the customer is NOT what *love* looks like in sales. There are many preconceived notions about sales consultants, and almost all of them fit into the above perceptions. To differentiate yourself, and to *love* sales, you need to be truthful, supportive, efficient, understanding, and attentive. Following the LOVE Sale Framework™ will help you embrace these concepts and *love* sales.

Questions to Consider

1. Which of the love types were you the most and least familiar with?

2. How do you think knowing about love will impact how you engage with your customers?

3. Do you have a philia relationship with any of your customers? If so, why? If not, why not?

4. How does agape love change your perception on love? How do you think it applies, or does not apply, to sales?

5. When did you feel tricked or swindled during a sales transaction? How did you respond?

6. When someone is wrong, how do you respond?

7. How do you address or respond to confrontation?

8. When did you have someone who completely wasted your time? How did you handle it?

9. When did you waste someone's time? Were you aware of it?

10. Name that person who you know who has diarrhea of the mouth. How did you know? How can you be mindful to let the customer talk and not talk to fill space or nerves?

11. When have you intentionally, or unintentionally, lied to a customer? What was the outcome?

12. How can you work to be known as a person of integrity? What specific area can you work on to improve?

7

Integrating the LOVE Sales Framework™ into Your Sales Process

There are many different sales processes that you could potentially follow. Ken Davis has *Getting into Your Customer's Head*; there is The Challenger Sale Model, Integrity Selling®, SPIN Selling, Miller Heiman, Dale Carnegie, Situational Selling, and many others. The LOVE Sales Framework™ can fit into any sales process you are already familiar with or studying.

One specific process I remember involved standing in a room with blue sheets hanging all over the walls. Each sales consultant in the company had filled out an oversized sheet with their key targets, champions, anti-champions, stage of the sales process (above the funnel, in the funnel, or best few), and timelines to close the deal. Then, the rest of the sales team members would critique and ask as many questions as possible about the blue sheet to help move the sales process forward and identify strengths and weaknesses.

To *love* sales, you will need to *love* communication, understand where to find business, appropriately measure your performance, and work on continually improving your skills. The LOVE Sales Framework™ can help you through each of these steps. Let's explore these areas together.

Communication

There are various resources available on how to communicate effectively. We have spoken earlier about how you can communicate by expressing emotions, making decisions, communicating a vision, collaborating, and sharing ideas. Strong communication skills are absolutely imperative to be a highly successful sales consultant. Can you make it by with so-so communication skills? Yes. But you will not *love* sales, delight your customers, or bring as much value as possible.

INTERNAL COMMUNICATION

What is your drive to get up in the morning? In his book *Start with Why*, Simon Sinek does a great job highlighting the importance of knowing your why to help guide your decisions. Sinek says The Golden Circle "Helps us understand why we do what we do" (Sinek 2011, 38). The Golden Circle concept describes three concentric circles with the WHY in the middle, followed next by HOW, and the outer circle is WHAT. Sinek argues that "Very few people or companies can clearly articulate WHY they do WHAT they do" (Sinek 2011, 39).

My challenge to you is to understand your personal why. Sales can be a very lonely job. You may have lots of windshield time, phone time, or waiting time to see people. You will get told no every day—multiple times per day. You will be laughed at. You will be sworn at. You will be kicked out and asked to not return.

People do not like to change, and as a sales consultant, your job is to be a change agent for your customer.

If you do not know why you get up each morning to endure these challenges, you will not have long-term success—or *love* sales.

Take time right now, put the book down, and spend five minutes on your why.

If you already know it, write it down and read it to make sure it fully captures your beliefs. Consider re-writing it as a personal mission statement. Having it written down and visible will remind you of your why after a hard sales call, mean customer, or just an overall challenging day.

If you need help uncovering your personal why, let's use these questions to get started:

1. **Reflect on your values:** What are your core principles and beliefs? Why are these most important to you?
2. **Identify your passions:** What gets you genuinely excited? What makes you feel fulfilled? Why?
3. **Look Back:** When you were going through school, playing a sport, or involved in a group, what experiences did you enjoy and why? How did these shape your personal why?
4. **Ask:** Take time to ask a friend or loved one how they see you. What qualities, actions, or traits do they admire? How does this align with how you see yourself?
5. **Use the 5 Why's:** Write down a goal or question and then keep asking why to get to a deeper understanding of the topic or motivation. For example:

    1. Why is love important?
        i. it costs nothing to give
        ii. it is unconditional.
    2. Why is being unconditional important?
        i. you don't need a fancy degree to earn it
        ii. you don't need a position to apply for it
        iii. it's freely available.
    3. Why is love being freely available important?
        i. there's nothing to buy
        ii. there are no gimmicks
        iii. nobody is disqualified from it.
    4. Why are no gimmicks important?
        i. it is authentic
        ii. it is genuine

     iii. it can have a lasting impact.
    5. Why is authenticity with love important?
      i. it embraces the core of who I am
      ii. it aligns my motives with my message.

In conclusion, *love* helps me align my motives with my message so that I can show up authentically with others.

6. **Consider your own personal self-talk:** Is it positive? Upbeat? Negative? Deprecating? How you communicate internally to yourself is just as important, if not more important, than how you communicate externally to others. If you have a negative view of yourself or your abilities, how are you going to be able to think positively with your customer? If you already think you have lost the sale or don't have a chance since this customer has never bought before, you are starting from a place of defeat.

Values

_____

Passions

_____

Reflect

_____

Ask

_____

Five Whys:

1   3

_____   _____

2   4

_____   _____

                                         5

                               _____

Personal Self-Talk

_____

Congratulations on building or refining your personal why. As you continue to refine how you can improve your own internal self-talk it is important to consider embracing a growth mindset.

In Carol Dweck's book *Mindset*, she talks about the difference between a fixed mindset and a growth mindset, saying, "You have a choice. Mindsets are just beliefs. They're powerful beliefs, but they're just something in your mind, and you can change your mind" (Dweck, 2017, 16).

A fixed mindset believes that one's abilities are innate and unchangeable (Dweck, 2017, 25). These types of people may avoid challenges or fear failure. They may say, "Why try?" if the outcome already looks like it is determined. People with a fixed mindset may give up easily, too, when situations get challenging (Dweck 2017, 99).

A growth mindset embraces challenges and sees failure as opportunities for learning (Dweck 2017, 99–100). People with this mindset believe that intelligence and abilities can be developed through hard work and dedication (Dweck 2017, 10). A common phrase you may hear from someone with a growth mindset is the term "not yet," meaning that even if a goal hasn't been reached, progress and learning are part of the ongoing process (Dweck 2017, 53, 61). This is critical in sales when every "no" becomes "not yet" as you learn the customer and ask questions to better understand with little wins in each call to provide overall value while building those emotional connections.

To *love* sales, you must know your why and embrace a growth mindset. If your internal self-talk is negative, how are you going to remain positive in front of a customer? If your internal ambition is low, how are you going to aim high with your goals? If your internal motivation is lacking, how are you going to motivate a customer to change? Continue to embrace, or develop, your why. Find ways that you can see the positive side of the situation, not the negative. Soon, those challenging sales calls will be celebrations of growth versus a reason to give up.

EXTERNAL COMMUNICATION

How you communicate with your customers will define how much they enjoy working with you. The most successful sales consultants I have worked with were excellent communicators. They made sure to keep the customer informed throughout the sales process and thought about what the customer might want to know. Let's explore a few areas to consider when connecting with customers.

Follow-up

Staying informed during the buying process is important. Keeping the customer informed after the sale is even more important! They have just purchased from you, they are excited to use your product or service, and they want to know details, timelines, and more. Information is readily available for us as consumers every day. We can track our packages, check on our ride-shares, see who has read our messages on social media, and even track our food deliveries straight to our door. Your customer expects the same level of service from you. Actually, they expect even more from you since you are a differentiated consultant.

When I first started in sales, I would travel directly to those customers that I was trying to close. I would drive for hours and past other customers to get to the ones that were buying. I would go through the sales process with that prospective customer and then head home. As I was learning in my early sales days, I didn't give my current customers the time or attention they deserved.

In Kevin Davis' book, *Getting Into Your Customer's Head*, he talks about being like a farmer to your current customers. Just like a farmer who goes around and tends his crops to make sure they are healthy, free of disease, and going to produce a good harvest, you need to be doing the same thing for your customer (Davis 1996, 244–245). You need to check back in with your customers to make sure they are happy with your product or service, that the competition is not in your account trying to build feelings of buyer's remorse, and that they are going to provide long-term value for your company.

One of the little wins that I would focus on in my territory was my ability to keep my customers. Each time I visited a current customer, I would do temperature checks in various areas. I could then use this information to see if the customer was doing well or if I needed to be intentional to spend some additional time with them in the coming weeks. Keeping up regular visits where I would talk with them and listen for ways I could serve them or bring additional value was one way I built follow-up into my daily routine.

Competition

You must listen to your customers to understand which of your competitors are in an account and what they are talking about! Early in my career, I sold against a very good consultant. She was always with my customers and planting seeds of doubt. When we competed head-to-head, we would split the account wins 50/50. At conferences, we would say hi to each other and grin, knowing that we were both going after the same accounts, on the same timeframe, with different resources.

She made me elevate my selling game. She created great competition. I was able to put a face with the name that I heard in my accounts daily. She challenged me to become a better communicator, better at follow-up, and better at uncovering customer needs.

She had a much smaller territory than me. This made it easier for her to follow up with the same customer. She was also more local to the region, so she had more regional knowledge about the customers and the area. I knew she was going to be in her territory every day, planting seeds of doubt about me, so I had to up my game!

With this information, it was even more critical for me when I closed a sale in her territory that I was regularly with my new customer. Remembering the farmer, I made sure to be in my new fields each week, at a minimum, so that the vultures did not come and ruin my newly planted crops! I made sure to find a reason to connect with various stakeholders at the account on a daily and weekly basis. I would also intentionally drive out of my way to service and follow up with that account to hear what was going well and what areas needed improvement. I did not want my lack of communication with my customer to hurt my future chances of making the next sale.

To *love* sales, you must embrace competition.

Staff

When you make a sale, make sure you know everyone who is impacted by your product, service, or idea. The person who signs the contract may be different than the decision maker, who may be different than the end-user. In a highly complex sales environment, there are often multiple different people who will use your product or service, and it is your job to understand each of them and how they feel about your product. Make sure to:

- Check in with the end-user to see if there are any issues with expectations or usability.
- Check in with purchasing to make sure they are pleased with your value.
- Check in with your decision maker to thank him/her for the sale and remind them of the value that you are providing to help his/her staff and operations work more effectively.

If you only visit the same person each time you are checking in, you will not totally convert the account.

Think again of the farmer; if he only checks a portion of his crops and then assumes that the rest are good, he may end up with a very bad crop. Be intentional to stop in and visit all relevant departments and stakeholders to make sure everyone is satisfied.

The larger the organization, the more difficult this can become. When I closed a six-hospital system sale, I had to train over 1,000 nurses across six hospitals, with locations in the emergency room, Post Anesthesia Care Unit (PACU), Neonatal Intensive Care Unit (NICU), psych ward, and multiple outpatient clinics. I had to check with purchasing and receiving at each location to make sure they were getting the product and were able to reorder smoothly.

I had to work with biomedical engineering to make sure any damaged or non-functioning products were being fixed quickly. I had to identify any potential long-term issues or design challenges that needed to be reported back to corporate. I had to check in with the end-users on very busy floors, with restricted access, and very sick patients (who were their top priority) to make sure I was bringing value quickly and hearing any concerns. I followed the mantra of "be brief, be bright, be gone" to cause the least disruption to their day as possible.

Selling to a smaller organization can be more simplified when the owners are wearing many hats. This can also make the follow-up more challenging since the staff is pulled in many different directions and doing multiple jobs at once. When I sold to mom-and-pop pharmacies, the structure was much smaller. Usually, the owner was the purchaser and end-user.

Communication was critical, no matter the size. The mom-and-pop pharmacy still thought they were the most important customer, and each of the six hospitals thought they were the most important when it came to service and time spent with them. Being clear about why I was there helped me be the most effective at following up and driving new business.

To *love* sales, you must understand how to communicate with the appropriate people to share your ideas and follow up appropriately.

Referrals

Consider this a two-way street. When you are communicating with your customer, you are asking them what is working well and asking who else you should speak with. If your customer is happy, they will give you specific people in their network that you should connect with. Treasure that name because you earned it, and your customer trusts you enough to share it.

If you sell to that referral and do a horrible job, it will get back to the person who gave you the name. Because the customer trusted you enough in the first place, it is your responsibility to make sure that you bring the same level of service and responsiveness to that new potential customer.

Referrals can be a true differentiator in your *love* of sales. Referrals usually want to talk with you because you are recommended by someone they trust. Just like you will likely try a new restaurant because a good friend recommends it, a prospective customer will likely have a meeting with you because their trusted peer told them the importance of it.

To *love* sales, you must be willing to ask whom you should also speak to and treat those referrals like gold.

New Information

To *love* sales, you must *love* to learn. You must take the time to understand new concepts and find what is relevant to your customers. As I progressed through my sales career, I realized that I was talking with more senior leaders about complicated finance and business operations. This was not my area of expertise, so I knew something needed to change for me to have credibility with these customers.

Therefore, I decided to go back to school and get my Master of Business Administration (MBA) in Finance and Healthcare Management. This would allow me to better understand how senior executives think and act upon information. I would learn the importance of financial ratios and how they correlate to profitability, how a managed care organization structure could impact customer's profits, and how accruals and capital acquisitions function. Without this knowledge, I could not effectively communicate my value through a long sales cycle and very complicated capital purchases.

After earning my MBA, my credibility increased, leading to better conversations with my customers. Now, my personal expertise has become a differentiator for customers when they perceive the product or service as "equal" to competitors.

You are valuable. Your knowledge is unique. Your customers want to learn from you. What will you teach them?

Do you need to get an MBA to be successful? No.

Do you need to continue to learn to bring value to your customers? Yes.

Only you know what is right for you, your goals, and your situation. Some things to think about:

- Are you going to be the expert in technology and how to apply it to your industry?
- Are you going to get a certification to help market and authenticate the service you provide?
- Are you going to attend a seminar where your customers also go so you can learn the same information and be able to talk about it together?
- Are you going to practice a particular skill (like communication) to improve each of your interactions?
- Are you going to take an online or in-person class to get better in an area your customer values (i.e., finance, marketing, operations, etc.)?

Be intentional in thinking about how you want to differentiate yourself in your market.

I challenge you to answer this question: "When my customer thinks of me as their sales consultant, I want to be known for _____."

You identified it, now go do it!

PRIORITIZATION OF TASKS

"I'm running around like a chicken with my head cut off. I drove for two hours to the farthest east part of my territory, and then I had to drive for three hours south to help a customer over there, and then I had to drive north to solve a customer situation. I just don't have time to prospect for new business since I'm driving all the time."

Of course, you have never said anything like this because you are a meticulous planner and master time manager. False! You definitely have said something like that and recognize that it is easy to get caught in the priority of the urgent.

Early in my career, I had a sales manager who would ask me various questions to help improve my sales acumen. One day, during a field ride, he asked me questions on prioritization that forever impacted my sales career. Let's see if you can pass the test.

Scenario: It is a normal day in the field (is that even true?!). When you stop at your first account, you have four requests that require your attention. The requests are:

1. You have a customer who has called and left a message that they need an in-service on your product.

2. You have a customer who called to place an order for your product.

3. You have a customer who has called to complain about a credit issue and needs it resolved immediately.

4. You have a customer who has called to voice a product complaint.

Here is the question my manager asked me: **"Which one of these should you do first?"** Now, you may tell me there is no right answer to this question. Each of these is important and critical to getting the sale. Yes, each of these is critical, but there is a clear winner. Have you picked your answer yet?

The correct answer is #2: Place an order for your product for the customer. Did you get it?! If not, let's explore why this is correct. Lots of sales consultants want to help by serving their customer. Three of the examples require extensive help by in-servicing the customer, working through a credit issue, and understanding the product complaint. However, the lesson my manager taught me will hopefully stick with you throughout your successful career and help you *love* sales.

He said, "The reason for placing the order first is because it directly contributes to bringing in revenue for the company. Without revenue, the company cannot fund the development of new products or support your sales salary. If you handle all of the other "issues" before the customer order, you're not prioritizing the company's revenue or your own pay. Always, always, always place the customer's order first. Your title is 'sales consultant,' not 'service consultant,' so place the order for the sale and then handle the other situations."

I know, I hear you. You may not like this response because it may be hard or inconvenient. However, it does help you understand where to spend your time. If you have an order in hand yet continue to work on "helping or serving" your customer, that order is not contributing to your sales quota or the company's bottom line.

When it comes to prioritization of tasks, think first of high-priority tasks (like order placement) that contribute directly to hitting your sales goal. As you filter the requests that will repeatedly come at you, you will need to determine their level of urgency and the amount of visibility it has within the organization.

As a sales professional, you are always on display to leadership with your sales opportunities and how you are tracking towards your objective. To *love* sales, you must prioritize your activities and responsibilities appropriately.

Time Blocking

Whenever I coach sales consultants, I always ask them when they complete their paperwork activities, such as follow-ups, expense reporting, and more. Successful sales consultants can clearly describe the time they set aside to complete these activities, whereas struggling sales consultants often don't have a plan for paperwork or prospecting.

A method that can help keep you on track is called time blocking. Time blocking is the process of scheduling blocks of time to complete certain activities (Hakoune 2019). You should have time for prospecting, follow-up, service, selling, proposal creation, ideation, and much more. As you look at your business, determine how much time you need to complete those tasks and then implement them into your schedule.

I'm not going to be popular with sales managers by saying this, but there is a certain amount of office work that needs to be scheduled in order to be effective in the field. I had sales managers who would say to me, "You cannot be in the office after 8 AM or before 5 PM each day. Work in the evenings and the weekends to get the rest of your work done so that you can maximize your time with customers." My challenge back to them was that I would be more effective if I leveraged office time to focus my time on the right customers at the right time to have those conversion discussions.

In one of my sales jobs, Monday morning was the best time for me to complete paperwork. The offices I sold to were just opening after the weekend, and the staff was busy checking emails and getting ready to see clients for the day. Unless there was an urgent issue that I was bringing to their attention (value to client), I usually stayed home for 2–3 hours on Monday morning to plan my week.

It is important to understand that when your customers have their busiest times, you should do your planning. Sometimes that could be Wednesday afternoon, or Friday morning, or Tuesday midday. There is no standard time slot to do office work. Look at your territory and monitor when the best time is for office work.

There is a flip side to this, too. There is an optimal time for prospecting or follow-up conversations. For one of my jobs, I discovered that this time was either right before or after lunch. Those I spoke to just before lunch usually needed a break from their morning, so they were willing to chat with me. Other customers liked it when I came after lunch since they were fresh again from their break. There is no right answer or time here. Each client is going to be different on when they want you to visit or call. You need to spend time learning about your customers and when they want to be connected with you and then appropriately block your time to meet with them during their value time (not yours). Meeting your customer when they want to connect will help you *love* sales.

Darria Long gave a great TEDxNaperville talk on "Triaging your 'crazy busy' life." As an Emergency Room (ER) doctor, she has to triage where and how she is going to spend her time. The four triage zones she mentions are:

1. Red: immediately life-threatening.
2. Yellow: serious but not immediately life-threatening.
3. Green: minor.
4. Black: items you must take off your list.

She mentions being in "crazy mode" is not an option when it comes to saving patient's lives. Crazy mode is when you're always busy, stressed, and reacting to all challenges in the same way. In her talk, she describes how to move from crazy mode to ready mode. This is where you "expect and design for crazy. Half of handling crazy is how you prepare for it" (Long 2020). Darria also mentions planning. A key factor of knowing where to spend your time and blocking categories is all about planning your time.

Daily Planner Time Blocking

TIME	ACTIVITY		TIME	ACTIVITY
6:00			2:00	
6:15			2:15	
6:30			2:30	
6:45			2:45	
7:00			3:00	
7:15			3:15	
7:30			3:30	
7:45			3:45	
8:00			4:00	
8:15			4:15	
8:30			4:30	
8:45			4:45	
9:00			5:00	
9:15			5:15	
9:30			5:30	
9:45			5:45	
10:00			6:00	
10:15			6:15	
10:30			6:30	
10:45			6:45	
11:00			7:00	
11:15			7:15	
11:30			7:30	
11:45			7:45	
12:00			8:00	
12:15			8:15	
12:30			8:30	
12:45			8:45	
1:00			9:00	
1:15			9:15	
1:30			9:30	
1:45			9:45	

If you struggle with planning your time or knowing where to spend it, keep a log to identify where you are spending your time. Make a chart, like the example below, with 15-minute increments for the entire day, and literally keep track of everything you do. Customer visits, drive times, meals, watching TV, conversations, sleep, and more. It should be everything you do during the day so you can get a good picture of where you are spending your time blocks. The more detail you provide, the more you will learn about your patterns, habits, and opportunities.

If you find that between 12 and 1 PM you are eating lunch by yourself, could you adjust and try to eat with a customer? Are you waking up at 7:30 or 8 AM and going to bed at 11 or 11:30 PM at night? Could you adjust your schedule to be more productive? Are you driving for 6–7 hours a day and only seeing two or three customers? Could you be more effective and intentional in your driving times?

Once you know where you are spending your time, you can adjust and leverage it appropriately.

Consider your tendency to over- or under-commit to activities. Know yourself, and if you are an over-committer, be intentional to block time to regroup. If you are an under-committer, think of areas where you can put yourself out there so you complete one more task than you think you should. There are extremes in this category. Find what works best for you, not anyone else, just you. You must be the one to commit to it and keep it running.

To *love* sales, you must be in command of your time and block it appropriately.

Communication
You may be picking up a theme here: communication is a critical skill when it comes to sales, and a big part of your success and ability to *love* sales will be time management.

- If you do not let the customer know what time you will be meeting them, how can you be upset if they are not there?
- If you do not let your manager or peers know what activities you are working on, how can you be upset if they do not see the value you bring?
- If you do not follow up in a timely manner with your customers on the items you discussed in your meeting, how can you be upset if they don't respond quickly to you?

You must master the ability to manage your time and communicate the required actions.

You will *love* sales if you know when you are doing certain activities. Getting to the end of your day with a full inbox, lots of texts, or 15-plus follow-up items on your to-do list can feel overwhelming. Having set times when you are communicating with clients and internal stakeholders will give you direction and focus.

One way to help you speed up your communication process is to use templates. If you know common questions or follow-up actions, you can spend time crafting a great message and then use that going forward. This can then be tweaked before sending it to another customer instead of having to re-write it each time. You will find what works and what doesn't work when it comes to customer engagement and responsiveness, and you can adapt your template to what gets the most open rate with your customers.

Remember, if you say you are going to do it, do it.
Do your best. Do it in an appropriate timeframe.

Responsiveness times can vary, and what is deemed acceptable changes over time. In the best-case scenario, when your customer asks for information, find out what their timeframe expectation is, confirm if you can meet it, and then let them know when they should expect to receive information from you.

After you have sent it, be intentional about following up appropriately, too, in case there are additional questions or information requested.

Effective time management separates the great consultants from the good consultants. Be intentional as a sales consultant to learn where you spend your time, what actions are priorities, and the right way to follow up with a customer. These skills will take time to develop, are very transferrable between jobs, and will help you *love* sales.

Where to Find Business

TARGETING

"If you don't know where you're going, all roads lead there." That is what my father always told me. It is extremely relevant in all areas of life, but it is especially relevant for you to *love* sales. Having a clear plan to know what business you should be targeting is critical for success.

As a new sales consultant, I thought that being busy and driving to all my customers would be what made me successful. As I continued to hone my skills, I realized that visiting my customers was important, but being focused on *who* I was visiting was just as important. My company used an A, B, and C rating for customers:

- A customers were the largest customers with the most dollar potential and highest market share availability.
- B customers were smaller customers but still had high dollar potential and moderate market share availability.
- C customers were the smallest customers with smaller dollar potential and a very low market share to capture.

You will notice that it takes relatively the same amount of effort to close an A, B, or C customer. When you consider the little wins you must identify, followed by the open-ended questions you must ask the various stakeholders, then the value you must provide to the customer, and finally, the emotional connections you must build to close the sale, this equals a lot of work!

For example, let's say you have a quota of $1,000,000. You have 12 months to achieve your goal. Where do you spend your time? You have five A customers worth $2,000,000 each. You have 10 B customers worth $1,000,000 each. You have 20 C customers worth $250,000 each. There are many different combinations that you could choose to pick to hit your goal. You could focus on 1–2 A targets only, five B targets, 8–12 C targets, or a combination of all three. If there are so many options, how do you decide where to go? That requires research.

RESEARCH

Understanding which customers are worth your time requires spending time researching them. This includes looking up information about them and asking questions to understand their buying process and willingness to try new things. You need to understand if you can convert part or all of the business. If you can convert 50% of an A target, you may hit your number depending on the overall size of the account. You also need to know your product or service niche. Do you have an area that would allow you to have an advantage over your competition?

When I sold point of care instruments, I had a clinical advantage. I believed, and could usually demonstrate, that my product was superior to what my customer was currently using. During my research, I needed to understand customers who were more focused on data and outcomes. Some customers were focused on ease of use or integration into their health system. Those customers were still targets but not my primary targets. By doing my research, I was able to focus my time on the customers who were more data-focused, and I had a higher likelihood of closing the sale since their ultimate buying decision would be clinical.

Let's go back to our example. Now, I can better segment my A, B, and C customers to know which ones focus more on data to make buying decisions. Let's say only one of the A targets is data-driven, three of the B targets are data-driven, and four of the C targets are data-driven. I've now narrowed my overall potential available market and can make a better-informed decision on where to spend my time.

Another key piece to research is to know the people who are your potential customers. Are they open to change or looking for the latest trends? Did they recently make a large purchase decision, and so they are hesitant to go through another large purchase? Did their leadership team just change, or have they been there for a long time? All these factors will affect your timeline for closing the deal. To make the best decision on where to focus your time, you need to consider one more thing—referrals.

REFERRALS

Referrals were mentioned in the communication section, but they also play a critical role in helping you to know where to focus on potential customers. If you have a current A customer who gives you a referral for another A or B customer who is interested in adopting the same type of product/technology, you will have a much higher potential closing rate. This will help you understand if you will be able to hit your quota number. This also helps you to know where to spend your time.

These three focus areas do not guarantee that you will close the sale or hit your quota. However, if you leverage them within your sales process, you will learn to *love* sales more because where you spend your time will result in more sales and better customer relationships.

Metrics for Success

I enjoy learning about how coaches are successful. Like him or not, Nick Saban, the retired head coach at the University of Alabama, has done a great job in his career to build and coach winning football teams. In *The Leadership Secrets of Nick Saban*, author John Talty describes one of the ways Saban is successful, which is by following "The Process." Talty says, "The Process really came down to discipline...everyone in the organization having the discipline to avoid the things they knew they shouldn't do and do what they knew they should even if they didn't want to" (Talty 2022, 91). To *love* sales, you must do things you do not want to do to be successful. One of those is to spend time to understand the metrics to guide your success.

LITTLE WINS RECAP

Earlier in Chapter 2, we spoke about focusing on and celebrating little wins, like your first order, a successful cold call, or handling a tough objection. Little wins are an important part of metrics. How you decide your little wins will determine if you are spending your time in the right areas to have success. For instance, if your metric is to meet with five customers each day, and you do that, are you going to hit your number? That depends. Did you align your conversations with those accounts identified above to help you drive your sales?

We also discussed setting realistic goals and expectations, including:

1. Know your numbers.
2. Break down your goals.
3. Prioritize your efforts.
4. Make your goals time-bound.
5. Adjust as necessary.

It's important to have a good understanding of each of these areas when it comes to metrics so that you are moving in the right direction.

A good way to remember metrics is to think of it like canoeing, where you must steer on the side of the canoe for the direction you want to go. For instance, if you want to go left in a canoe, you need to row on the left side. However, if you continue to row on the left side repeatedly, eventually, you will go around in a full circle. You will have exerted a lot of effort and seen new things, and you will be moving, but you will not be making progress.

Some sales consultants get caught in the rut of calling on the same people, in the same accounts and talking about the same things. This is equivalent to rowing only on the left side of the canoe. To make it into new waters and see even grander sites, you must row on both sides of the canoe to keep it straight. You must be calling on many different stakeholders, including those who do not want to meet with you. You must target and capture new customers by proactively reaching out to them instead of waiting for them to call you.

*Your ability to identify the right metrics, paired with your personal effort level, will directly affect your ability to **love** sales.*

Being in a canoe is fun. Going around in circles in a canoe is fun for a short period of time. Going around in circles in a canoe for a long period of time is frustrating and irritating. Let's explore how we can straighten out your canoe to help you enjoy your sales journey.

UNDERSTAND YOUR MARKET AND WHAT DRIVES WINS

It is probably self-evident, but every market is different in the way it operates. However, people are relatively similar. People across all markets have emotions, meaning you can connect with them regardless of your industry. You must find what drives the people at your accounts to say yes to the sale.

The "yes" person, or team, will be different account-by-account. This makes the industry or market irrelevant to metric success. If you have a product that solves a particular challenge, then you need to find the people within that account who would be impacted by the challenge. If you sell a service that people could use, you must identify why those people would be interested in that type of service and then approach them accordingly. If you have an idea, you must find the people who are open to hearing and acting upon ideas.

There have been many books written about customer types, and I'm not going to go into great detail here. Remember that everyone is different and that some people like to:

- make quick decisions
- make slow decisions
- have lots of data to make decisions
- make a gut reaction with no data decisions
- make sure everyone likes the decision before moving forward
- over-analyze decisions
- stall decisions from fear
- embrace change as good
- fight change as bad
- talk about change but never take action.

As you can see, there are as many styles as there are people. Asking questions will help you understand the different types of people you will be encountering and how to best set metrics to connect with them.

You will need to think about your territory metrics:

- Do you need to drive for longer distances to reach the right number of customers to make sure you hit your number?
- Do you need to make a certain number of phone calls to make sure you hit your number?
- Do you need to have a certain number of samples or supplies available to demo or sell in a given timeframe?

All these areas are things to think through versus just waking up and heading out the door to "go sell something today!" Figure out the best day for you to put a plan in place for the upcoming week. You can reframe your work week to a Wednesday-to-Wednesday work week, and then your "Friday" becomes Wednesday so that you are able to take valuable sales action on the days that your customers are available. Your planning day can be more of a local day with calls in the morning to available customers and then in the afternoon to check off all the items you will need for the next week.

You will *love* sales if you have a plan of where you are specifically going to go and what you are going to accomplish.

TOOLS

There are many sales Customer Relationship Managers (CRMs) to track all kinds of activity. No matter what your company officially uses, you should have your own process of keeping track of your activity.

When I first started in sales, I bought a paper map of my territory and used push pins to chart my entire territory. I used green pins for current customers, red pins for competitive accounts where I had no access, and blue pins for competitive accounts who would see me.

Building this map helped me to get an overall view of my territory and plan my activities and routes better. I then used this map to scout out visiting my green customers 1–2 times per month, my blue targets weekly, and the red targets at least once each month.

There is no right or wrong method here. I have met many successful sales consultants who used many different tools—the key is having a tool to use.

No matter what the tool is, in its most basic form, you must track who you are talking to, what their interest level is, and how to categorize them. The key is that you are doing the work to categorize your customers.

Take note: if you do not track your customer engagements because you think you will remember, you will not. Try to remember what you had for breakfast four weeks ago. Our brains are only good at storing information for a short period of time, and we need systems to help us remember so that we don't have to use that brain power to store the information.

As Antoine de Saint-Expuéry says, "A goal without a plan is just a wish."

To *love* sales, you must embrace using tools to help you know when and where to go.

RE-EVALUATE YEARLY AT A MINIMUM

As with anything, sometimes you need to re-focus your efforts to achieve maximum results. This does not mean your current method is wrong, outdated, or ineffective, it is just a realization that you need to be evaluating your methods to maximize your performance. What worked yesterday may not work today and may not work tomorrow.

You need to embrace the mindset that to be the best, you must continually re-evaluate.

I recall once when I had a great sales year. I had a large funnel of opportunities, my customers were happy, and I was well on my way to hitting quota like I had the year before. However, inside, I felt something was off. I did not feel I was operating at my peak performance. I stepped back and started to look at all the areas where I was focusing and tried to identify areas where I could improve.

I realized that the organization of the materials I provided to customers was not streamlined. I would spend too much time looking for certain material. So, I threw my system out and started over from scratch. I re-thought what materials I would need and what items contributed to having successful calls.

For those other collateral items that I needed but didn't leverage to grow business, I put them in a separate area and kept less stock. This meant that as I planned out my week, I could quickly look through my new organization system and see where I was running low on supplies. It also helped me gauge how active I was in accounts that would drive sales for me by the amount of collateral I was giving out (little wins).

This change did not directly impact my customers or coworkers; it only helped me. It made me more effective and prepared for my sales calls. As I had success, I was able to share my method with others who were interested. My manager did not ask me to reorganize. My peers did not prompt me to reorganize. Internally, I realized that I could be better at organizing my items to make me the most effective sales consultant for my customers.

Being able to identify your why, as mentioned earlier, will clarify the driving force within you. If you need help, ask someone who has been successful to shadow you for a day and provide suggestions on how you could improve. Keep in mind that they will share based on what has worked for *them,* not for you, so you must evaluate if their method will work for you.

Everyone has ideas and works in certain ways, but only you can determine how you will work most successfully. Allow yourself time to step back and evaluate your metrics. Consider how they are helping or hurting you to reach your goals. Think about what steps you can implement to update your metrics for more success. Also, think of the little wins you can focus on to determine if your own personal metrics are accurate and forward-focused.

Communication, focus, and metrics are important to *love* sales because they will help make sure you are on track to hitting your goals.

Measuring and Analyzing Sales Performance

Before the end of the year, I had to sell 1,000 boxes of product. Each box cost $1,000. I know you just did the math; yes, that is $1,000,000 in sales. That was my quota. And everyone else in the entire country's quota for the year. It did not matter territory size, location, number of customers, demographics, sales consultant tenure, or total available market—every territory had to sell $1,000,000 of product in the calendar year.

I hear you; this doesn't sound fair! Large city territories could hit that number a lot quicker than the more rural territories, for sure! (Of course, I had a rural territory.) This was a new product the company was launching, and they had made a commitment to sell a certain amount of product to the supplier. To be able to meet the supplier commitment, each territory needed to sell $1,000,000 in year one. Did sales consultants complain? Of course! Did people miss their number? Yes. Did people hit their number? Yes.

Let's get something straight—if you are in sales, you are going to have a quota.

To *love* sales, you must learn to embrace your sales quota. Most of the time, the quota is going to be hard to attain; it may be unrealistic or feel completely overwhelming when you first receive it. To be successful and *love* sales, you will need to take the time to measure and analyze your sales performance so you can know if you are on track or off track to hitting your quota.

You will *love* sales if you hit your quota. You will make money, get recognition, and have strong customer relationships. It will usually feel good both internally at your company and externally with your customers. Even with hitting or exceeding your quota, it will never feel perfect. Acknowledging that it will be challenging with certain customers or internal processes is part of embracing the sales process. Let's explore a few ways you can measure and analyze your sales performance to *love* sales.

KEY PERFORMANCE INDICATORS (KPIS)

If you work for a company, you are going to have an annual review with certain metrics you must achieve to gauge your performance. However, what if your own metrics are different than what you get in your review?

I challenge you to think of your sales territory as your own personal small business. No matter the size of the company you work in, you can run your sales territory like you would your own small business. You are the CEO of your territory, and you can make the decision on where and how you spend your time and resources. But first, you must understand what you are tracking so you can measure your performance effectively.

That's where Key Performance Indicators (KPIs) come in. Notice it doesn't say APIs (All Performance Indicators). It says **key** performance indicators. Therefore, you need to pick those metrics that will best align with you hitting your sales objective or quota. We spoke earlier about different metrics you can measure, but let me ask you a few questions to help you make sure you are on track:

1. Think about how much revenue or sales you have generated Month to Date, Quarter to Date, or Year to Date. How is that tracking towards you hitting or missing your quota?
2. What is your close rate or conversion rate with customers? Do you win one out of two or one out of 10 sales? This will help you understand how much time and focus you need to put in to capture the right amount of activity to drive to those close rates.
3. How many leads are you generating, and how many of those are converting to sales? Do you have an active pipeline that is fed to you by data? Do you have to find your own customers? When you connect with a prospective customer, how often do those conversations lead to converting customers? You need to study your market and customers.
4. What is the average size of your sales conversions? Remember our A/B/C level targets? Do you know how many accounts you need to close to be able to hit your quota based on your average account size?

QUICK FACT: A $120,000 account for the year will only be worth $60,000 six months later since you will lose $10,000 each month. Therefore, the faster you can convert the business in your calendar year, the more potential revenue you will receive from that customer throughout the rest of the calendar year.

5. What is your average selling price (ASP) for your product or service? The higher your ASP, the quicker you can attain your quota.

QUICK FACT: In my earlier example, if I sold each box for $1,000, I would make my $1M quota with 1,000 boxes. However, if I dropped my price to $750 per box, I would need to sell 1,333 boxes. The lower my price goes, the higher the number of units I need to sell to make the same amount of profit.

6. How many customers do you lose in a year? (This is also known as churn.) Can you maintain 100% of your current business in a calendar year? If not, you need a plan to account for customer attrition to hit your overall objective.

QUICK FACT: If you have a $10,000,000 territory with a $1,000,000 quota but lose 20% of your customers per year, you are going to have to sell $3,000,000 worth of product to hit your objective ($2M churn + $1M Quota = $3M total)

Each of these areas can contribute to the KPIs that you should be measuring. The KPI will vary by business or account type, but if you don't know the answers to the above questions, you are going to have a hard time knowing if you are going to hit your number or not.

SALES METRICS, CYCLE LENGTH, AND WIN RATES

There are many different sales models available to track where your customer is in the buying process. Are they ready to buy now, buy later, or not interested at all? Certain methodologies mention Above the Funnel (>12 months to close), In the funnel (6–12 months to close), and Best Few (90 days to close).

This is not the only way to track. However, you should have short-, medium-, and long-term sales funnel metrics that you can measure to see how long it takes your customers to go through the buying process. As you evaluate the funnel metrics, you can get a sense of the effectiveness of your sales process.

Having customers in the "above the funnel" category for years means that you need to re-evaluate that type of customer. The same is true for your "best few" accounts. If a customer has been on the best few list for six or more months, there is something going on with your customer or sales process flow. If you don't measure it, you won't know it, and you'll regret it.

As part of this analysis, you should see your average sales cycle length. Can you close a deal in three days, or does it take you three years? Depending on your business type, target customers, size of the purchase, the complexity of the sale with the number of stakeholders, and a host of other factors, you will see variability in how long it will take to close the deal.

For perspective, I worked on a large four-hospital health system deal that generated over $2,000,000 in revenue, but it took me 12 months to close the sale. To do this, I was on-site with the customer each week, working with various stakeholders to gain alignment to move forward. The longer it takes to close a sale, the more prospects you need to have available in your funnel to hit your quota.

Another area related to measuring your performance is knowing your actual win rate. If you have 20 opportunities in the year and you only close two, that's a 10% win rate. However, if you can convert eight out of 20 opportunities, that's a 40% win rate. The higher your win rate, the more effective you are at converting prospects into customers over a period of time.

These metrics will be different for each person and industry as there are lots of factors to consider. However, if you do not take the time to see how often you are winning, you will go after customers and hope it will work out versus being more confident that you have the right number of opportunities in your pipeline based on your conversion success metrics.

REVIEW AND ADJUST

Your data will only be as good as how well you maintain it. If you do not take the time to put quality data into your CRM to track sales funnels, conversions, or churn, you will not have good data to leverage. The "back office" work is the most mundane (or boring) for sales consultants who want to be face-to-face with customers. However, those consultants who truly *love* sales learn how to leverage the data so that they can be successful with their customers and their companies and build long-term customer relationships.

Periodically, you will need to go back and review your metrics to determine that you are still capturing and measuring the most applicable ones. I cannot specifically tell you what the best metrics are for your market or industry, but I can recommend that you take time to study your customers and territory to find where you are having success. Work to understand why and then replicate that behavior throughout your territory to build lasting success.

Continuous Improvement and Learning

I hated going to school when I was younger. I didn't understand what was so great about it. The classes were boring, I didn't think the content was very relevant to my life, and I was never at the top of the class or winning awards. However, when I got to college, something clicked. I was in the Ohio University Marching 110, and one of their mantras was "better than the best ever." The work ethic, fun environment, and thrill of performance each week made me want to show up better and better each week. After four years of this type of mindset literally being drilled into my head, I graduated and then hit the sales world.

Like all new sales consultants, I struggled to learn who my customers were, where they were located, and what their interest level was in my products. As I would drive to accounts, I would listen to books, talks, sermons, and sales-related content to help me improve. Little did I realize that I enjoyed those long drives because it gave me a lot of time to learn about different people, strategies, or ideas that I could then leverage.

Continuous improvement and learning helped me *love* sales since I was constantly growing my skills and being able to practice them with customers. Let's explore a few ways you can embrace continuous improvement and learning to help you *love* sales, too.

SET LEARNING GOALS

Just as you set specific goals within your sales territory, you need to be clear on what goals you want to focus on for your own learning. Do you:

- want to ask better questions?
- become a better negotiator?
- improve your cold calling?
- grow your presentation skills in front of people?
- more boldly advocate for your product or service?
- embrace overcoming failure and rejection?
- learn more about industry trends?

There are so many resources to help you begin your journey on any of the above topics. You can read books, listen to podcasts, join organizations, take a certification class, go back to school, hire a coach, or leverage a peer or internal program.

However, the key to understanding where to begin is to know what you want to achieve. What do you want to learn? Just as we talked about SMART Goals during our discussion on little wins, you can apply SMART goals to your learning goals, too.

Let's say you want to improve and ask better questions. What should be your goal? How would this fit into the SMART goal-setting framework? Let's try it:

GOAL: Learn one new open-ended question a week and practice with three close customers

- **Specific**
  - ☐ *Evaluation:* The goal is specific, indicating that you want to learn one new open-ended question per week and practice it with three customers. It provides clarity on the type of questions to focus on.
  - ☐ <u>Verdict:</u> Specific ☑

- **Measurable**
    - □ *Evaluation:* The goal is measurable as it specifies the number of questions to be learned (one open-ended question per week) and the number of practice sessions (with three close customers).
    - □ <u>Verdict</u>: Measurable ☑

- **Achievable**
    - □ *Evaluation:* The goal seems achievable, as it involves a realistic and manageable task—learning one open-ended question per week and practicing with a reasonable number of customers.
    - □ <u>Verdict</u>: Achievable ☑

- **Relevant**
    - □ *Evaluation:* The goal is relevant, especially since my goal of improving my questioning skills is aligned with my broader objectives and development plan for my sales career.
    - □ <u>Verdict</u>: Relevant ☑

- **Time-bound**
    - □ *Evaluation:* The goal is time-bound as it specifies a timeframe of one week for learning a new question and practicing with three close customers. It provides a clear deadline for when I want to achieve the goal.
    - □ <u>Verdict</u>: Time-bound ☑

<u>OVERALL VERDICT</u>: *SUCCESS.* This goal fits well into the SMART goal model because it is specific, measurable, achievable, relevant, and time-bound. All these factors will increase your likelihood of achieving this goal. Plus, if you do this for a year, you will end up with 52 new open-ended questions that you can try with your customers.

Remember,
no learning goal = no direction = no intentional growth.

Stop reading right now and write down two goals for yourself when it comes to what you want to accomplish in sales.

GOAL 1:

_____

GOAL 2:

_____

Great! Now, how are you going to hold yourself accountable for achieving them? (Yep, you must write it down.)

I will hold myself accountable for achieving my sales goals by:

ACCOUNTABILITY FOR GOAL 1:

_____

ACCOUNTABILITY FOR GOAL 2:

_____

Be bold with your learning goals. To *love* sales, you must be ambitious in setting learning goals for yourself.

INDUSTRY ENGAGEMENT

Your market is unique. Your industry is unique. It is up to you to learn everything you can about it. Here are some steps to guide you:

- attend conferences to stay updated
- read online about influential people in the industry
- learn and understand why they are important
- study past events to gain insights
- anticipate future trends and developments
- explore emerging trends in the industry
- research key people shaping the field
- look into various organizations or societies
- note regional/national meeting schedules
- ask your customers what they read
- ask your customers what events they attend
- understand why they read or attend those things
- be curious about your customers
- be curious about your market
- be curious about your territory
- be curious about your industry.

Let's be real, this is going to take time. You are not going to become an expert overnight in a particular industry or market. You will need to take the time to research, ask questions, and network with key players throughout the industry. As you continue your sales journey, you will learn more and more that will help you set yourself apart from other sales consultants. You will *love* sales because you are expanding your knowledge of the industry and will be able to bring more value to your customers.

FEEDBACK

I love asking the question, "How can I improve?" I had a manager who always told me that "feedback is a gift, both to give and to receive." Most people hear the word feedback and think it is going to be negative, but that does not have to be the case. Feedback is not about what you are doing wrong; it can be about what you are doing right and what you should continue to leverage and improve. You may not *love* the feedback you receive, but if you hear it with *love* and an open mind, you can probably find what is trying to be said.

As a sales consultant, you will often hear people complain about your product. This feedback is a gift—it reveals the key objections you are going to hear about your product. When you start hearing complaints about your competitive products or services, it's an opportunity to improve. You now know how to sell against those even better than you did before. Taking that information can help you craft better questions, provide better service, and give better feedback to your company to make better future products or services.

When my managers would come and ride in the field with me, I would always ask them for feedback on my performance at the end of the day. Usually, the answer was trite, "You did a good job today. Keep up the good work." Blah. That is a cop-out answer for a sales manager. When you become a manager, do not give that type of advice.

To help me get more actionable feedback, I would ask them, "What is one thing you think I did well today, and what is one area you think I could work on?" This would solicit a much better and more detailed response.

Timing was also key to this conversation. If I asked my manager when he was getting out of the car to catch a plane at the airport, I could not expect the feedback to be very detailed. To overcome this, I would ask for feedback after a specific account visit, during a meal, or well before we had arrived at the airport so he had time to think.

Feedback can also come from mentors who help you along the way. If you have another co-worker who is willing to help you grow or practice, you will get tremendous feedback. It will be a lot harder to fool your mentor, and you can get any nerves out of the way when you ask those "dumb" questions.

I also leveraged technology to help get feedback. Every sales consultant in the company had a program on their phone that they had to use each day for continuous learning. The program would have scenarios posed in the form of questions, either written or verbal, and then the sales consultant would have to answer in the best way possible. A neat feature of the program is that sales peers could provide feedback on the other sales consultants' answers to let them know if they were on track or not.

The app provided real-time feedback from fellow field experts to elevate everyone's selling acumen. The app also improved the culture of the whole sales team by giving and accepting feedback to raise everyone's level of performance.

Ultimately, you will have to be willing to hear, digest, and respond to the feedback you receive. If you keep the mindset that feedback is a gift and can help you improve versus an attack on your skills, you will learn to *love* the art of improving your selling skills and making sales.

SALES SCENARIOS

I can already see your eyes starting to glaze over, and you may want to skip this section! As sales consultants, we hate having to do sales scenarios. I've heard so many complaints, including, "They aren't realistic," "The person I'm selling to doesn't know the right objections," or "I don't really need to practice. I just need to learn to carry on a good conversation." Wrong. You do need to practice. You are right; sales scenarios are not realistic; the real thing is much easier. And yes, having good conversations is a part of sales, but how do you move the customer to action and not make your sales call just a nice chat? This comes down to practice. You will not *love* the practice, but you will *love* the result.

Let me challenge you to embrace a mindset shift around selling scenario practice.

If you can sell your product, service, or idea to someone who knows nothing about your industry, market, or customers, you will definitely be able to sell it to anyone in those areas. Why? You must be extremely articulate, clear, and engaging to keep someone who knows nothing about what you do interested! Leverage your friends, family, spouse, kids, or anyone else who will listen to you to practice your message.

Let's think about the ultimate purpose of selling scenarios—to practice asking better questions and prepare for various situations. If you practice your craft to ask engaging, open-ended questions, you will get the customer talking. Be intentional about trying questions and seeing how your partner responds. Did the question make sense? Did the conversation go smoother or go off the rails? You can even get your partner to intentionally throw you objections or attitude so you can prepare for various situations.

It will feel awkward.

Your partner will probably laugh at you.

Trust me, this won't be the last time.

One of my most memorable selling scenarios came after I had been promoted to a sales training position after being in the field for many years. To help my new sales consultants learn to handle objections, I created an exercise called Toastmasters. Each sales consultant in the class would walk up to the front of the class, stand behind a podium, and then have to answer a random sales objection asked by an expert in the back of the room.

The goal was to practice overcoming objections, simulating the pressure of being "on stage" with a customer, and hearing different approaches to handling objections. To add additional pressure and objectivity, an "expert" panel, including senior consultants, leaders, and our national sales director, was present at the back of the room. These experts would vote after the objection was handled and determine if the consultants passed (green card) or failed (red card).

I was proud of the game, and it was working well. However, during my first class, my national sales director threw me a curveball. After the class had finished their objections, he turned to me and said, "Okay, Paul, your turn behind the podium, and I'll ask the questions." As I was new in my training role, my reputation and credibility were on the line! If I didn't know how to sell and overcome objections, why should the class still trust me to teach them?!

Like any good leader, I led by example, accepted the challenge, and walked up to the podium. What happened next was rapid-fire, random objections from my national sales director at me. I handled each one and saw green cards (thankfully) rise from the expert panel. Instantly, I gained insight into how my learners might feel, which better prepared me to give feedback to the class. It also solidified the importance of practicing to become "gameday" ready.

Is Toastmasters a realistic simulation of what will happen in the field? No. However, the objections that we practiced, such as, "Your price is too high" or "This product is the same as the one I'm currently using," are the exact same objections the consultants would face in the field. Those who embraced the exercise usually did well once they got back to their territories. They recognized the importance of continually honing their skills through practice.

Just like any good athlete, musician, or chef, the more you practice your craft, the better you become. Keep practicing, keep failing, and you will *love* the sales results you achieve.

Developing a Personalized Sales Approach

"You do you" is often interpreted as the act of making decisions based on one's beliefs and being true to oneself. Just like we spoke about in Chapter 5, I like to boil this down to being your authentic self.

The LOVE Sales Framework™ is built to help you do you! You can adjust and leverage each aspect of the framework to what fits you best. You can create your own goals and questions, determine your own value, and build your own emotional connections. You can determine how you best communicate, prioritize, and measure your performance. You can analyze, track, and improve in the ways you want to improve. All I ask when you do you is that you DO IT!

You are unique. Nobody is like you. You have certain strengths and skills that you can use to be successful and connect with customers.

Just like you, each customer is unique. What works for one customer may not work for another. While your sales message may be the same, remember that people are different. Each person is unique and will make decisions in different ways.

Personalize your sales process for each customer while you do you, and you will *love* sales!

Questions to Consider

1. How is your internal self-talk? Positive? Negative? What ways can you continue to improve it?

2. What is preventing you from practicing selling to peers, mentors, or others? Who can you practice with regularly?

3. What continuous learning goal did you set for yourself? What steps will you take to achieve it?

4. Which mindset, growth or fixed, do you embrace most often? How can you improve?

5. How do you prioritize your time and activities? What is something you need to adjust or improve?

6. What SMART goals are you going to make for yourself to achieve in the next month, quarter, and year?

7. How do you target and track your opportunities? What additional research or referrals do you need to get to be successful?

8. How do you feel when you receive feedback? Do you see feedback as a positive or negative? Why? Who is someone who can give you actionable and accurate feedback?

9. What KPIs do you currently measure?

10. What KPIs stood out as important to you?

11. If you could create your own KPI, what would it be and why?

12. What tools do you use to track your engagement? How do you reevaluate to make sure you are still on-track?

(8)

Building Confidence and Resilience

"You need thick skin to be in sales." I hear this comment all the time. Sales is a difficult but rewarding profession. You have high highs and low lows. There is the thrill of closing the sale, and there is the rejection of losing the sale. There is the adrenaline rush of talking to that prospect, and if they say yes, it will change your life. And there is the uncertainty of where the next sale is coming from to make ends meet. I have experienced both the highs and the lows. To *love* sales, you must develop your confidence and resilience.

This is not a quick process. You will need to practice a new mindset every day. Scroll on any social media platform, and you will see messages about mindset and reframing situations. In sales, your ability to control your mind, see the situation for what is really happening (and not happening), and develop how you personally will respond will define your ability to be successful in sales long-term.

Overcoming Sales Rejections

You are going to lose. I have not met a single salesperson who has won every single sale. You are going to get rejected. You are going to feel upset, mad, frustrated, infuriated, puzzled, angry, furious, and more. But you must realize and accept that rejection is part of sales. Rejection hurts emotionally. Accept that it will happen. How are you going to prepare for when rejection happens?

FOCUS ON THE PROCESS, NOT THE OUTCOME

I love to challenge myself physically to remain fit and able-bodied. That is why I signed up for a Spartan Race to test my abilities. Spartan prides itself on not telling the participants what obstacles they will have to face until they arrive on race day. This mindset helps the runner focus on the training process rather than training for the specific obstacle they are going to have to overcome.

This was helpful for me when I began training. I did upper body, lower body, grip strength, flexibility, strength exercises, bear crawls, and more to prepare for any obstacle I may face. My overall fitness level improved with each work-out. My form improved with each workout. Over the course of three months, I worked out multiple times per week and focused on the process of getting stronger, faster, and more flexible.

Come race day, I felt prepared for whatever obstacles were in my path. As I went through the course, I would approach each obstacle with all my effort to see if I would pass or fail. Passing felt great! A total adrenaline rush! One of my challenge areas in training had been the monkey bars. During my Spartan Race, I completed the monkey bars! Check. Mission accomplished.

There were other obstacles that I had not trained for that were much more challenging. The rope climb, if you have never learned to do it with a J technique or another way, is very challenging to just "show up and finish." However, with some brute strength and some minor cuts later, I hit the cowbell at the top of the rope.

Then, at the very end of the race, right before I had to jump over the fit pit, I ran up to the multi-Rig. This is a combination of rings and bars that you need to swing across without touching the ground to get to the cowbell on the other side. I approached this obstacle just like all the rest. I prepared mentally, shook my arms for some blood flow, and stretched my hands to awaken my grip.

First ring, good. Second ring, got it. Third ring, yes! Fourth bar...what?! I dropped. I didn't have enough momentum to make it to the bar section. Hitting the ground, I grabbed my two 20-pound kettlebells and did my penalty loop out and back through the muddy and uneven woods. After that detour, I jumped over the fire pit and finished my first Spartan Race!

This is a book on sales, so why am I talking about exercise? The Spartan Race is a good example of embracing the process over the outcome. My overall goal was to finish the race. However, I did not complete each obstacle successfully. In sales, your ultimate goal is to bring value to your customers and make sales.

Each day is a workout.

A practice session with a new question, an opportunity to have a difficult conversation, a chance to work on prioritization skills, or a chance to deliver a better customer experience than the last time. Ultimately, these practice workouts are the steps you take along the way to continue to perform your best. Some of the Spartan obstacles were easier than others, just like certain accounts and sales will be easier than others.

The race is a great example of overcoming rejection:

- Did my moves look as good as others? No.
- Did I pass all the obstacles? No.
- Did I embrace what was in front of me? Yes.
- Did I ultimately finish the race? Yes.

Rejection, when broken down into little opportunities versus major events, will help you recognize that not every customer will be the right fit for your product or service.

Rejection will teach you that each time you get rejected, it offers a chance to learn about yourself, what you could improve, and the type of customers you connect with.

Rejection will teach you how to improve. It will force you to learn from your mistakes. It will make you question your process. It will make you focus on what went wrong. Maybe you think that rejection equals failure. Time for a mindset reframe—rejection equals learning. You could do everything exactly as you have done before and still get rejected. You could try new questions and have great dialogue and commitment and still get rejected. You could have an incredible idea that will significantly change a person, process, or product and it will still get rejected.

In the midst of this rejection, it's important to take the time to learn from it by asking reflective questions and focus on ways you can continue to improve:

- Did you lose because of a poor relationship with the customer?
- Did you not ask enough open-ended questions to all necessary stakeholders?
- Did your negotiation skills fall short?
- Did you skip a part in the sales process because things were going so well, and then that came back to hurt you in the final moments of the sale?
- Did you break trust or not hold yourself accountable for the actions that needed to be done to win the deal?
- Did you enjoy rest instead of hustle?
- Did you embrace grit, or give in to an easy path?

Rejection will help you—if you let it. Remember, selling is a process, and you must embrace and enjoy the process of selling your idea, product, or solution, not just the result of getting the order. To *love* sales, you must embrace rejection as learning and reflect, reframe, and retry—often.

EXTERNAL FACTORS TO REJECTION

There will always be factors beyond your control that can contribute to rejection. For example, I had a hospital customer who was very close to buying my product. I had completed all the required sales activities, asked good questions, showed value, built emotional connections, and was a front-runner in the buying process. However, I lost.

When I went back to the customer to ask for ways I could improve, they told me that the competing rep lived in the area and was well-connected with a lot of the people in the account because their kids were on the same sports teams and involved in the community together. I lived three hours away, and I did not have kids. Those were factors completely out of my control, but they significantly influenced the outcome of that sale.

You are going to have times when you cannot control the environment, the people, or the buying process, and you are not going to get the sale. In those moments, you will have a choice. What are you going to do next? Are you going to complain about how unfair that customer was or about the outcome? Or are you going to pick yourself up, brush yourself off, and go get the next sale?

Knowing that factors outside of your control will happen to you will help you realize that you can still *love* sales without being able to control everything. You will also need to build resilience.

Building Resilience

Knowing that rejection is part of the sales process, you need to learn how to build your resilience for when you will experience rejection. Reactions like hitting the steering wheel, having road rage, and taking your anger out on others are not good coping mechanisms. Let's explore a few strategies that will help you *love* yourself and remind you why you *love* sales.

COPING MECHANISMS

I cannot tell you the exact thing that will help you cope with rejection. I'm not a therapist, nor do I intend to try to be one in this book. Since each of us is an emotional being, we each have strong emotional connections and responses to various things. I will challenge you to explore the list below and find ways that you may be able to leverage certain items to cope with rejection in a healthy, positive way:

- exercise
- breathing/mindfulness activities
- start/stop/continue a hobby
- journal or write about your experience
- create art
- go out or talk with friends and loved ones
- practice positive affirmations of your skills
- express what you are grateful for instead of what you lost
- take a break from technology
- spend time in nature
- have a routine to follow
- talk with a counselor or therapist
- leverage a coach for skill development
- read a book
- find time to laugh
- go to the beach
- volunteer or help others
- spend time with family
- color

- try sensory exploration or positive visualization
- drink coffee or tea
- go to a show, play, or movie
- attend a workshop.

This is not an exhaustive list, but being mindful of how you can best recharge after rejection is critical to *love* sales long-term. Review the list above and write down three ways you can be intentional to prepare to cope with rejection. You already know you will experience rejection; therefore, it is important to have an action plan in place. Start writing below:

Coping Mechanism #1:

_____

Coping Mechanism #2:

_____

Coping Mechanism #3:

_____

One of the things that worked for me was listening to sermons and audiobooks (fiction and non-fiction) during my drives. I would also listen to music that created positive memories or got me energized for the next meeting. I would be intentional to take my camera into nature and get some great photos. I would spend time watching the ocean or enjoying the sunset to see something beautiful versus thinking about my rejection. Just because it worked for me doesn't mean it's going to work for you. Be deliberate to take time to explore the best ways that you rejuvenate and get back into a more positive mental state.

SUPPORT GROUP

There is power to saying something out loud and writing it down. Find trusted colleagues, mentors, friends, or family with whom you can share your experiences. Allow yourself the opportunity to vent. We all have moments where we need to express frustration about something. It's important to have people in your life to be able to share your frustrations with who will listen, not judge, and not spread what is said to others. This may take work, but find a person, maybe a therapist or coach, who would be willing to listen to your challenges and be judgment-free so that you can move forward in the situation.

Allow yourself time to vent, but also realize when venting becomes complaining.

You can start to wear down your resistance with too much negative talk, so:

- Find co-workers who spur you on to be better rather than tearing you or the company down.
- Find mentors who challenge you to reach new heights versus mentors who just encourage you to share more juicy gossip details.
- Find family members and friends who will truly listen, love, and support you instead of someone who is only interested in hearing the drama so they can pass it on to the next person regardless of the impact it will have on you or the situation.

Sales can be a very lonely profession. To *love* sales, you must surround yourself with people who will listen and encourage you to continue on your journey.

PATIENCE

Patience is hard. As emotional beings, we are wired to get what we want quickly. We live in a time when information is constantly at our fingertips. Search it or say it, and you can probably find it in milliseconds. However, when it comes to developing relationships, working through contracts, and closing sales, patience is necessary. You still need to actively follow up with your customers during the sales process, but you must be patient and work with them as they make their decisions.

The Bible offers great wisdom on the importance of having patience:

"And let us not grow weary in doing good, for in due season we will reap, if we do not give up." Galatians 6:9 (ESV)

"But you, take courage! Do not let your hands be weak, for your work shall be rewarded." 2 Chronicles 15:7 (ESV)

"Love is patient and kind; love does not envy or boast; it is not arrogant...Love bears all things, believes all things, hopes all things, endures all things." 1 Corinthians 13:4,7 (ESV)

Ask any sales consultant how long it takes them to close a sale and they'll tell you it takes much longer than they want or expect. This is where patience is so important. Just as close relationships, skills, and habits take a long time to build, learning patience takes time and effort too. Patience is required to find the right questions to ask, where to find value for the customer, and when building meaningful connections.

You must be patient with your customers. You need to spend time with them, be curious about them, and look for ways to enjoy your time together. You likely won't make a sale the first time you make a sales call to a new customer.

There are many caveats to the speed with which you will make a sale. You must consider the cost of your product, the market you are in, and where the customer is in their buying process. There are many more variables, but you get the picture.

Patience and resilience go hand-in-hand. If you are not resilient, you will not keep showing up. If you are not patient, you will not wait for what is going to come.

Think of a time you had to complete a class or were earning a degree. How long did it take you? Most of us go through six years of primary school and then six years of secondary school to get a high school diploma. Next, you may choose to go to post-secondary school and attend a two- or four-year college or university to get an associate or bachelor's degree. Some may continue even further through Master's and/or Doctorate level programs, which take additional time to complete.

Regardless of whether you enjoyed the journey, you had to be patient to reach the end prize. You do not get a Master's degree after one class. You do not get a bachelor's degree after one class. You do not get a high school diploma after one class. We are trained early in life to be patient for the big things. However, when we get into sales, we expect instant gratification!

Think of building your *love* of sales like attaining a doctorate degree versus watching a TikTok or YouTube video. The process is going to take time, but the result will be worth it. Plus, you will have a lot of learning along the way as you embrace being patient for the result.

EMBRACING OPTIMISM

In Chapter 7, I mentioned Carol Dweck's book *Mindset*, so I'm not going to summarize it again here. However, it is worth mentioning that Angela Duckworth, in her book *Grit: The Power of Passion and Perseverance,* also mentions a growth mindset. Duckworth proposes that challenges are seen as an opportunity to grow, and abilities can be developed through perseverance and hard work. There are many other books available about building and fostering a growth mindset. So, how does this relate to sales?

When I think of sales and a growth mindset, I primarily think about optimism. When you are asking people to change behavior, routines, products, or more, you are going to get resistance. That resistance will come at you from all angles all day long. I did not have a day in sales where there was not some situation or concern that needed to be addressed. It could be a situation with a customer on credit hold when they were trying to place an order. Or a big sale just got stopped because a truck broke down and the delivery did not arrive.

Or there was a major snowstorm, so the patients who were going to get the product did not come to the office. I could go on and on. Ask any sales consultant who has been in sales for longer than a month, and they could share the various stories and obstacles they have faced on any given day.

What makes those long-tenured sales consultants successful and continue loving their sales job? Optimism.

Their motivation behind why they are optimistic may be different. Some may stay optimistic because of the amount of money they could make when they close the deal. Others may be optimistic about the recognition they will get from the company when that big deal finally closes. Others will be optimistic because they realize the impact their product or service had on a particular person and how they had a chance to impact a life positively that day. Still, others may be optimistic because they are looking only to a short-term goal (i.e., if I do this for the next six months, I can leave and do something different). Others may embrace optimism as part of the journey and see every opportunity to develop their skills, deliver value to the customer, and provide an exceptional experience regardless of what obstacles are in their path.

Those sales consultants who truly *love* sales embrace each conversation, experience, and challenge as an opportunity to grow, learn, or engage.

Being optimistic also relates to how you view yourself and your abilities. Do you see yourself as being able to be successful in sales? If you said yes, you are probably very optimistic that you will be able to convince a customer to try your product or service. However, if you said no, you may have a lower view of your ability to be successful in sales and may struggle with finding ways to be optimistic in front of your customers. Companies spend lots of money on training to help sales consultants learn the products, but optimism is an intrinsic motivation that cannot be obtained with product-filled training.

To grow your optimism, you must practice being optimistic. Here are some examples:

- When you get rejected, smile.
- When you get cut off in traffic, think kindness.
- When you lose a big opportunity, think of what you did well in the process.
- When someone else wins Sales Consultant of the Year, congratulate them.
- When you miss the luxury trip by one spot, congratulate the person who did win.
- When you're having a bad day, and the person you're talking to is having a great day, smile even though you don't want to.

The great thing about optimism is that it is a choice. Your manager doesn't have to force you to be optimistic. You will probably not have "be optimistic" written in your Goals and Objectives for the year.

You have the choice every day, in every interaction, to choose if you will look at it positively or negatively.

Yes, your prospect said they would see you but then had to cancel at the last minute after you drove hours to see them. At least they were willing to make an appointment with you. Maybe their delay was because they were working on a larger impact project or action. Or, they may have just wanted to get rid of you because you have the word "sales consultant" in your title. With a slight reframe, you can become optimistic and call on that same customer again to showcase the value you can bring to them.

I remember an incident I had with a customer when I walked up to the window and asked to see the office manager. I knew she was there because as I was walking up, I saw her talking to the receptionist. As I approached the desk, the office manager quickly walked away and motioned with her arm in a push mo-tion of "no way" to the receptionist. When I asked the receptionist to see the office manager, her response to me was, "She's not in today."

That was a total lie. I knew it, and the receptionist knew it too. I did say that the office manager told me she was in the office on this day and to stop by any-time. The receptionist stuck with her lie, and I was not going to have a meeting that day. Was I frustrated? Yes. Was it wrong to lie to me? Yes. But I chose to be optimistic about the situation and think that that poor office manager must have so much on her plate that she couldn't take five minutes to talk with me even though she told me to "stop by anytime."

We are all emotional beings, and we make emotional decisions that are not rational. Get used to it. You are going to connect with some people and not with others. Learning to adapt and remain optimistic during those blatant disre-spectful situations will, with practice, make you an even better sales consultant.

I knew my worth in that office manager situation. I knew my product would have helped her, her office, and her patients. But she was not willing to have a conversation with me. Still, her very rude "no"—delivered by the reception-ist—did not indicate that she would never buy from me ever; it just meant not today. I still kept that office in my routine call pattern, and I would continue to brainstorm how to bring value to the receptionist and the office manager during each of my visits.

Each customer goes through the sales process at a different speed. What remained consistent was that I trusted myself, my selling process, and my abil-ity to ask questions and that I would bring more value than my competitors. Therefore, I just needed to remain optimistic and persistent to reach my goals since I knew it would take longer for the customer to realize those facts.

You see, a growth mindset focused on optimism in sales helps you to remem-ber that there is always a flip side to the situation. It may be difficult to find that flip side, and it may take time and practice. However, the more you intention-ally practice finding the positive and remaining optimistic, the more you will *love* sales.

Confidence Building Exercises

I always enjoy meeting people and learning their stories. At one particular meet-and-greet, a co-worker reached out and set up a time for us to have an introductory conversation. She had seen me in the halls and on social media. During the conversation, she mentioned to me that she thought I was so confident and that she wished she could be that way. I asked her a few questions to have her elaborate, and she talked about challenging situations in school growing up and how mean kids were to her. She felt her confidence was completely shattered and that she would never be able to be truly confident after those encounters.

I don't think she is an anomaly. How other people see us is very important. Are we competent, friendly, outgoing, smart, or funny? On the flip side, are we incompetent, unapproachable, shy, dumb, or crass? I haven't been able to find who said it, but one of the best quotes I have ever heard when it comes to confidence is, "Confidence is how you view yourself, not how others view you."

> To **love** sales, you must first love yourself and be confident in your own abilities.

One way to help you learn to be more confident is by following the LOVE Sales Framework™:

Little Wins: Have you set clear goals for how you are going to develop your skills? Do you look for ways to showcase that you are improving? Are you celebrating when things go well? Are you being specific in your goals?

Open-Ended Questions: Are you asking questions of others to find your areas of improvement? Are you curious about how you are perceived? Are you asking clarifying questions to understand the root cause versus the surface level? Are you actively listening to the answers?

Value: Are you thinking about and leveraging what makes you unique? Do you understand the value of self-confidence as it relates to sales? Are you having empathy for others as they give you "tough" feedback to make you better? Are you actively going to embrace the objections that come and be willing to hear them when you ask?

Emotional Connection: Are you willing to dive deep into self-awareness to learn your confidence? Are you willing to take an assessment or a class to get more familiar with how you can improve your confidence? Are you willing to embrace being authentic to who you are versus how the world sees you?

PRACTICE, PRACTICE, PRACTICE

This is not the answer you want to hear, but because I'm your sales coach, I'm going to tell you hard things. To get better at being confident, you must practice being confident.

Amy Adkins has a great four-minute video on "3 tips to boost your confidence," where she discusses that confidence comes from what you're born with (your genes), how you're treated (social pressures), and the choices and risks you take (Adkins n.d.). While we cannot control parts one or two, we can control part three. This is especially important in sales. You cannot control your genes or how you were treated growing up, but you can intentionally put yourself in situations that will help you increase your confidence.

Scan
to watch

Here are some tips:

1. **Practice negotiating a proposal:** The first time may not go so great, but the second, third, and so on will show an improvement.

2. **Practice asking open-ended questions:** Your first open-ended questions will likely be long and drawn out as you try to form the words. Your next ones will get shorter and more effective until you become more proficient.

3. **Practice listening:** Once you ask your open-ended question, listen for the answer. It is easy to listen to a close-ended question because you will hear "yes" or "no," and then it is your turn to talk again. A good open-ended question keeps the conversation going for quite some time, so you will have time to stay quiet and practice listening.

4. **Practice sales pitches:** Your first sales pitch will sound funny. If you practice, you will continue to get better. Don't know enough about your product yet to practice? Try selling your favorite hobby to a friend or loved one and see how it goes.

One of the best ways to *love* sales is to be gracious to yourself. Remember:

- If you are just starting in sales, give yourself grace—mastery is going to take time.
- If you are switching to a new industry, give yourself grace—it takes time to learn.
- If you are at the start of a new year and your quota is high, give yourself grace—everyone has the same amount of time to perform.

Confidence building can be strengthened through using the "Little Wins" in the LOVE Sales Framework™. The reason to have little wins is to help make you more confident along your sales journey. By hitting or surpassing your small goals, you will boost your confidence to hit those larger goals. Those little wins show that you are making progress, you are learning, and you are having success.

Remember how I told you I ghosted my customer because my competitor's car was in the parking lot? Yeah, not one of my finest moments, but I learned a valuable lesson that day in self-confidence. This turning point in my life was pivotal in helping me understand my "why" for showing up to accounts and that I would never be intimidated by my competition again. I had to improve my selling skills, embrace being confident in my abilities and products, and do the necessary activities to get the results that I wanted to achieve.

Staying Resilient in the Face of Sales Challenges

What is your why? Not why are you doing sales, but what gets you up and out of bed each morning? What is your internal "why" for your actions and behaviors? Are you only motivated to make money? Are you going into sales because you think it will be easy money? Are you hopeful to travel or meet lots of people?

In his book *Start with Why*, Simon Sinek says, "People don't buy WHAT you do, they buy WHY you do it....Knowing your WHY is not the only way to be successful, but it is the only way to maintain a lasting success and have a greater blend of innovation and flexibility" (Sinek 2011, 42, 50).

Let me be bold:

- If you do not know why you get up each day to go to your sales job, you do not know your why.
- If you encounter objections and don't push back on them, you do not know your why.
- If you skip that last cold call of the day, you do not know your why.
- If you are comfortable with your current customers and don't go after new customers, you don't know your why.

Until you define your why, you may have some success here and there, but you will not have lasting success. Your journey to find your why is going to require self-discovery. You are going to have to go deeper within yourself to define your why. Your manager, co-worker, peer, or friend cannot give it to you. Your spouse, loved one, or coach cannot give it to you.

Only YOU can dig deep and find your why.

Let's explore a few ways to help you find your why.

Reflect on your Values and Beliefs
What do you believe in your core? What are your core values? Family? Faith? Fun? Fortune? Fame? What is most important to you personally and professionally? What issues do you resonate with the most? Where, or about what, do you become passionate? What issues or values, when challenged, will cause you to fight the most?

Passions
When do you feel energized? Fulfilled? Excited? What activities, both personally and professionally, get that passion to show up? How do these activities bring you joy? How do they relate to your overall values or beliefs? How do your passions reflect your purpose?

Deep Questions
When was the last time you felt a strong sense of purpose or fulfillment? What was occurring? What feelings did it stir in you? Why? What legacy do you want to leave to your family, friends, co-workers, kids, country, followers, teachers, or more? What impact do you want to have? How are you going to go deeper?

I pursued a career in medical device sales because I was passionate about helping people. This cause aligned closely with my Christian faith. Plus, going into medical sales aligned with a dynamic, ever-changing, progressing, and necessary industry. I realized people would always get sick and need help! I wanted to make a difference in my world by helping other families have more time with their loved ones through the products and services that I sold.

On the days when I didn't want to get up and brave the cold New England winter roads, I thought of my parents. If they were sick or needed help, I would be on those roads in a heartbeat to help them. My love and care for my parents, and now my wife and kids, became the embodiment of why I would serve my customers no matter how I was feeling. My why for helping my customers meant that I would get up at all hours of the day, in all types of weather conditions, all to provide the necessary care.

EMBRACE THE CHALLENGE

You are going to have sales challenges. Read that sentence again. Now, read it out loud. The more you accept the fact that you are going to have sales challenges, the more ready you will be to understand your why so that you can overcome those challenges.

Your why does not instantaneously change your outcome, it just changes the perspective with which you approach it.

Remember my example of not showing up for the appointment earlier? That meeting fundamentally changed my why. I stepped back and realized that I did have something to offer; my products were excellent, and I could always continue to grow my selling skills. It may take me some time, but eventually, I will get better.

One of my early goals upon graduating college was to win Sales Consultant of the Year. It is a coveted award where you get a nice trophy, cash, trip, or other high-end reward. For me, it was a goal of reaching the top. Within five years of graduating college, I achieved my goal. I won Sales Consultant of the Year. The celebration was fun, the accolades were nice, and the trip was a bonus. But what I remember was the next morning. After breakfast, my leadership team came up to me and asked, "So, what deal are you going to close next?" Twelve months of hard work to win the prize, three hours of celebration, and then I was back into the "How are you going to hit quota for this year?" conversations.

Without having a why, that conversation probably would have broken me. I knew why I got up each morning to help my customers, so I knew the next sale I was going to close and the next goal I was going to achieve.

As you progress in your career, through sales or other pathways, your fundamental why (faith, family, etc.) will not change, but some of the little why's (Sales Consultant of the Year) change for the goals you set and why you want to reach them. You may want to leave a bigger legacy, have an impact on people, prove to yourself you can still accomplish that particular goal, or it just sounds fun, and you want to try it.

Learning to *love* sales is all about embracing failure as a learning, understanding and embracing your why, and building confidence to show up authentically each day with your customers. The journey to *love* sales does not happen quickly. It is a slow process, focused on little wins, open-ended questions, providing value, and building emotional connections that align with your why.

Questions to Consider

1. What is your why? How can you go deeper to find it?

2. What does resilience mean to you? How have you shown it in the past? How can you become more resilient?

3. What coping mechanism are you going to leverage to stay refreshed in the face of rejection?

4. Who would be in your support group? Why?

5. When was the last time your product, service, or idea was rejected? How did it feel? What did you do about it?

6. How are you going to practice, practice, practice to improve your confidence?

7. Where do you need to be more optimistic?

8. How can you practice being more optimistic in your day-to-day experiences? What situations are most challenging for you to be optimistic?

9. When did something out of your control impact you? How did it feel? How did you respond?

10. When is it hard to be patient? How can you intentionally practice being more patient?

11. Where do you need to have grace with yourself? What about grace with others?

12. What little wins can you create and remain accountable to help you increase your confidence?

13. As you explore your why, what values, beliefs, passions, or deep questions did you uncover?

9

The Journey Ahead

What a journey we have been on. If this is your first book on sales, congratulations on starting your sales learning journey. If you have read countless other sales books, thank you for giving me an opportunity to shape your skills. Now, the real journey begins. You get to put into action the LOVE Sales Framework™ and work through all the successes and challenges that come with the sales profession. From talking with countless salespeople throughout my years, the stories they can tell of their successes and obstacles would fill many, many books.

I hope you caught the word *journey* I used. A journey is less about the destination and more about where you go along the route. Journeys can also be of various distances. I have taken short day trips to the city, weekend trips to the country, vacations to the Caribbean, and a multiple-week trip to Europe. Each of these trips required planning but to a different level.

For instance, my wife and I were planning a road trip to visit friends over a holiday weekend. Everyone kept telling us the traffic was going to be horrible and it would take us much longer than we wanted to get there. We brainstormed plenty of ideas. Should we leave the night before? Should we drive through the night? Should we get up really early? Should we take an entirely different route? Or should we just leave at our usual time and embrace the traffic?

Then, we changed our perspective and talked about the journey we were going to take. We could drive for a bit and stop and experience a new area along the route. Maybe a coffee shop, a walk in a local park, or a unique food spot. You catch my drift. Our long, traffic-filled trip was now one where we could look forward to the journey and not just be concerned about reaching our destination on time.

Sales is very similar. Before we talk about the journey ahead, let's look back at what we've learned about the LOVE Sales Framework™.

Recap of the LOVE Sales Framework™

By now, you will remember that LOVE is an acronym representing actions within a framework designed to help you build confidence and equip you with the tools for success.

LITTLE WINS

We started by discussing "L," which stands for Little Wins. We talked about how little wins can help us set realistic goals and expectations within our sales process so that we stay motivated. This includes being very prescriptive about actions to take like getting an order for one product, handling an objection well, or getting a follow-up meeting. We realized we are not very likely to close the deal on the first appointment, so we need to set up our goals and expectations so we can achieve our goal.

Also, as part of the "L," we discussed celebrating our wins. Acknowledging and celebrating our wins helps us boost our confidence, track our progress, and build positive responses to challenging situations. If we are so focused on the bigger end goal, we can potentially become de-motivated by the other actions and tasks that must take place for us to be successful. By taking time to focus on and celebrate our little wins, we can increase our confidence in our abilities and pave the way for success.

OPEN-ENDED QUESTIONS

We next discussed the "O," which stands for Open-Ended Questions. Asking questions, in my opinion, is the most important skill a sales consultant can have. However, it is important to ask meaningful and conversation-worthy questions that stimulate dynamic responses. We have all met sales consultants who ask, "Do you like what you're currently using?" The answer is going to be yes 99.9% of the time. If the customer didn't call you, then they most likely enjoy what they are using and do not want to switch. Therefore, we spent some time showcasing different types of open-ended questions you can use to start a dialogue and not a one-way lecture.

We realized that when we use open-ended questions, we can better uncover needs and pain points, build rapport, and establish trust. We can better understand our customers by doing research before our meetings so that we can ask questions relevant to them, their business, their industry, and their competition. We also talked about the 5 W's and H question types.

After we asked our open-ended questions, we discussed the importance of active listening and our follow-up questions to clarify, confirm, and respond.

Lastly, we discussed how curiosity plays a role in helping us to ask better questions by focusing on what we can learn about the other person versus what we want to tell them.

VALUE

Next, we discussed "V," which stands for Value. Value is hard to define specifically because each person will assign value differently. Some people place a high value on how they feel. Other people value how much money they will make. There are also those who place value on how they will look to others (or themselves).

We discussed the importance of understanding a value proposition by focusing on ways you are unique and what you bring to the sales interaction. We talked about segmenting your customers and doing a competitive analysis. We also discussed how to identify customer needs and pain points through questioning, empathy, and feedback.

We discussed how to demonstrate the value of your product or service through customized presentations, success stories, and being a knowledge expert on your product or service. When we are building value with customers, we are going to encounter objections.

Remember that objections are good and convey that the customer is interested in what you are offering, but some questions must be answered before they are willing to commit. To bring value, you can focus on anticipating the types of objections you will hear, reinforce your value, and be ready to talk about price.

Another factor that sets you apart as a sales consultant is the value you bring to the customer, not only through your product or service but also through your unique qualities. Do not forget the importance that you as a person play in the sales process.

EMOTIONAL CONNECTION

Finally, we discussed the "E," which stands for Emotional Connection. We were reminded that we are all emotional people. We have logic, but we also have emotions. As a sales consultant, it is our job to sell to both the logical and emotional side of the buyer. We started by discussing emotional intelligence and how to be self-aware, self-regulatory, and empathetic. We talked through how to build trust and rapport with customers by being responsible, clear, communicative, and authentic.

We talked through empathy and being able to put ourselves in our customers' shoes to validate their emotions and tailor appropriate solutions for them (not for us). We also discussed how people use emotion to buy through fear and desire, storytelling, and positive associations.

Lastly, we talked through some examples of how to create an emotional connection with customers through personalization, follow-up and care, empathetic problem-solving, and surprise and delight. We realized that we can be very successful and *love* sales if we understand the motivations and emotions behind our customers and work to make our product, service, or idea valuable for them instead of for ourselves.

TYPES OF LOVE

An interesting component of this framework is the different types of love and how we embody each of them. We discussed an overview of *The Four Loves* by C.S. Lewis and the definitions of storge, philia, eros, and agape love. We discussed how our relationships are influenced by our family history (storge love) and how our friends (philia love) can be a good guide for our customer relationship. How passionate love (eros) does not have a place in the sales process, and how we have a greater, unconditional love (agape love) through a loving God.

We talked about what selling with *love* does *not* look like: tricking your customer, telling them they are wrong, wasting their time, having diarrhea of the mouth, or lying to them.

INTEGRATION OF THE LOVE SALES FRAMEWORK™ AND BUILDING RESILIENCE

We spent time talking about how we can put the LOVE Sales Framework™ into practice through communication, focus, and time management. We discussed where to look for business, how to define our metrics for success, and how you can make the LOVE Sales Framework™ your own.

We spoke about overcoming rejections to help with our resilience. We spoke about a growth mindset, embracing optimism, and confidence-building exercises to help us look introspectively at our self-esteem and how we can show up confidently for our customers. We highlighted the importance of our values and passions, and challenged ourselves to think deeply about how we are going to overcome the challenges of sales.

Whew, what a journey we have been on. Congratulations on wanting to improve. You have heard about the skills and ideas that will work, now it is up to you to practice.

Your Journey Ahead in Sales

As a reward for finishing my Masters, my wife and I booked a weeklong vacation in Aruba to relax after the intense two-and-a-half-year journey. We had never been to the island before, and we both love warm weather and beaches, so we thought it would be a good fit.

One of the day activities offered through the resort was a UTV ride. This vehicle looks like a four-wheeler with doors, a roll cage, an open windshield, and a full steering wheel. After we heard the safety discussion, we put on our helmets, jumped in the UTV together, and the group took off. As we progressed through our ride, about a third of the way in, we came to a spot where there were mud puddles. Some groups opted to go around them, but we were "all-in" for this trip. I revved the engine and headed straight into the huge puddle.

Immediately, a wall of brown water rose up in front of the UTV and proceeded to crash through the open windshield on both of us! We were absolutely *covered* in mud. I looked over at my wife to see her reaction, and all I could see were the whites of her eyes and teeth. Everything else was covered in brown mud. Thankfully, she was smiling, and so was I, so we continued our journey.

There were plenty more mud puddles along the way, and we intentionally went through each of them. Some people in our group avoided all the puddles and laughed each time we arrived as we became muddier throughout the trip. Finally, we reached the end of the tour, took our picture, and left the experience to go change and get the mud out of our hair, clothes, shoes, and more.

My wife and I went on the same journey as everyone else on that UTV tour. We all had the same terrain, vehicles, and obstacles along the way. However, my wife and I chose to take a route that made us dirty, provided a little more excitement, and created a lasting memory we still cherish!

Your sales journey is similar. The journey does not end when you close the deal, it just continues. The journey is about a continual learning process, finding opportunities for growth, and embracing the adventures that are ahead of you. Keep in mind that your journey will look and feel different than other sales consultants' journey—and that is okay.

Think of selling as a journey with no end date.

When you embrace the journey, you are accomplishing the following things:

PERSONAL GROWTH

A journey involves a continual process of learning. You will learn more about yourself and discover how you respond to excitement, fear, failure, and challenges. If you are willing to go on the journey, be willing to watch how you will personally grow through the process.

EMBRACING THE PROCESS

Each journey has some uncertainty. Just like those mud puddles on the UTV ride, you can choose to embrace going through the uncertainties and get a little dirty, or you can avoid them. If you embrace the uncertainties, you will build resilience and handle the next journey even better from your learnings.

APPRECIATING THE MOMENTS

You are going to have moments on a journey that are a blast and those that may not be as fun. Think of a road trip. While being in the car can be fun during parts of the trip, it can also be boring and uncertain if you hit traffic or don't have a charger for your devices. Just like with little wins, celebrate the milestones you achieve along the journey, and keep an eye out for key moments or experiences you can take with you. You will learn something from each sales process you go through, so remember all the moments and how each felt and what you can learn from them.

BUILDING CONNECTIONS

The UTV experience helped my wife and I grow closer in our relationship. We also built friendships with the other UTV riders as we shared an experience together. You will meet many people along your sales journey. Cherish those connections and enjoy the relationships you build. You may or may not cross paths again, but you can learn something from everyone.

MINDSET CHANGE

We talked earlier about the importance of a growth mindset. When it comes to your sales journey, you should always be thinking about how you are learning and growing. You should also take note of how you can reduce stress or anxiety when it comes to objections or roadblocks along the way. Fill your journey with optimism and see it as a way to grow, learn, and engage in new ways!

MAKING MEMORIES

Ultimately, journeys are made for memories. Memories can be positive or negative. Fun or sad. But the one guarantee is that you will have a memory. How will you embrace the sales journey as part of your story so that you *love* the sales process versus just focusing on the destination of closing the sale?

If you are looking to create a value-based, emotionally connected customer relationship that lasts, you need to embrace and remember the memories along the way. Memories are a powerful tool for sharing what you have learned with others. As you progress through your sales journey, you will use those memories to help the next generation of sales professionals start their own journey.

Embrace the journey, look for the areas you can grow, appreciate your customers and the experiences you are able to have together, embrace an optimistic mindset, and build memories. Just as during a road trip, you cannot control where there will be construction, an accident, or a lot of traffic; you just need to embrace the journey and be ready for whatever comes your way.

The Close

I still have a few questions for you to understand if you are truly sold on how important *love* is to the sales process:

1. What are you still concerned about with trying the LOVE Sales Framework™?
2. What questions do you still have on how to begin?
3. What objections do you have to this framework?
4. What will it take for you to embrace the LOVE Sales Framework™?
5. How will you know when you are ready to move forward?
6. What's preventing you from trying the LOVE Sales Framework™ and seeing the success you can have?

There are a variety of answers to these questions. There are also lots of emotions you may feel, like fear, excitement, anxiety, hope, uncertainty, confidence, dedication, trust, and many more. Only you can decide what emotions are holding you back from trying this process.

Only you can choose to make a change or not.

As I was practicing on my journey to become certified as an executive coach, the program taught me the importance of asking open-ended questions to let the client work through their situation. One of the questions that can be asked when a client is struggling by only seeing one side of a situation is: "And how could that be a good thing?" This helps the client think about the situation through another lens and see the other side of the situation.

For example, the client could say, "I didn't close that sale, and I really needed it to hit my number." The coach would then ask, "And how could that be a good thing?" This will make the client think about all the hard work they did as part of their sales process, what they learned, and how they are now better able to overcome objections. They may reflect on all the work they did on building relationships or even how they learned to prospect more effectively or better. There is no right or wrong answer here; the question helps to explore a different perspective and learning.

So, I ask you, "How can applying the LOVE Sales Framework™ in this book be a good thing for you?"

Final Thought

Sales is a tough profession. If you've stuck with me this long, you realize all the components that go into making a sale. It's rarely a show-up, throw-up, and close-it-up type of engagement.

My final thought and advice to you is to challenge yourself to have fun. Embrace the sales process as a game. Think of how the sales journey can be enjoyable. Create fun challenges for yourself to continually improve. Utilize your family, friends, or coworkers to support you as you grow your skills.

The more joy you find in the selling process, the more you will *love* sales. I hope you see that with a little more *love*, you can have a lot more sales.

Let all that you do be done in love.

1 CORINTHIANS 16:14 (ESV)

References

"A Quote from Chatterton." n.d. www.goodreads.com. Accessed December 29, 2023. https://www.goodreads.com/quotes/9149867-the-value-is-always-in-the-eye-of-the-beholder.

"A Quote from Just a Number." n.d. www.goodreads.com. https://www.goodreads.com/quotes/7926138-trust-takes-years-to-build-seconds-to-break-and-forever.

Abraham Jr., Kelvin. 2023. "Plot Diagram Definition & Examples." Study.com. Accessed January 12, 2024. https://study.com/learn/lesson/plot-diagram-overview-examples.html.

Adkins, A. n.d. "3 tips to boost your confidence." www.ted.com. Accessed February 28, 2024.

https://www.ted.com/talks/amy_adkins_3_tips_to_boost_your_confidence.

Duckworth, Angela. 2016. *Grit: The Power of Passion and Perseverance.* New York Scribner.

Dweck, C. (2017). *Mindset: Changing the Way You Think to Fulfill Your Potential.* London: Robinson

Frei, F.X. and Morriss, A. (2023). "Storytelling That Drives Bold Change."

Harvard Business Review. Accessed January 2, 2023.
https://hbr.org/2023/11/storytelling-that-drives-bold-change.

Gartner. (n.d.). "Definition of Pain Points – Gartner Sales Glossary." Accessed
January 28, 2024. https://www.gartner.com/en/sales/glossary/pain-points

Gitomer, J. 2004. *Jeffrey Gitomer's Little Red Book of Selling*. Sound Wisdom.

Mind Tools Content Team. 2023. "SMART goals." Mind Tools. Accessed
January 22, 2024. https://www.mindtools.com/a4wo118/smart-goals.

Gitomer, J. 2017. "People don't like to be sold-but they love to buy." Accessed
January 12, 2024. https://www.gitomer.com/people-dont-like-to-be-sold-
but-they-love-to-buy/.

Hakoune, R. 2019. "How to boost your productivity with time blocking."
monday.com. Accessed January 19, 2024. https://monday.com/blog/
productivity/increase-your-productivity-with-time-blocking-a-step-by-step-
guide/.

Harvey Mackay Academy. n.d. "The Mackay 66 Customer Profile." Accessed
January 12, 2024. https://members.harveymackayacademy.com/wp-
content/uploads/2018/12/Mackay-66_Updated-2018.pdf

Lee, Harper. 1960. *To Kill a Mockingbird*. Philadelphia: Chelsea House
Publishers.

Lewis, C.S. 1960. *The Four Loves*. San Francisco: Harperone.

Long, D. 2020. "An ER doctor on triaging your 'crazy busy' life." www.ted.com.
Accessed January 19, 2024. https://www.ted.com/talks/darria_long_an_
er_doctor_on_triaging_your_crazy_busy_life/transcript?language=en

Masterclass. 2021. "How to Use the 7-38-55 Rule to Negotiate Effectively."
Accessed January 6, 2024. https://www.masterclass.com/articles/how-to-
use-the-7-38-55-rule-to-negotiate-effectively.

Rice, E. 2019. "Listen to Understand Not to Reply." Norhart I Blog. Accessed December 24, 2023. https://www.norhart.com/blog/2019/01/18/listen-to-understand-not-to-reply.

Sinek, S. (2011). *Start with Why: How great leaders inspire everyone to take action*. London: Portfolio/Penguin.

Talty, J. 2022. *The Leadership Secrets of Nick Saban: How Alabama's Coach Became the Greatest Ever*. New York: BenBella Books

TED-Ed (2016). "How miscommunication happens (and how to avoid it) – Katherine Hampsten." YouTube. Accessed December 28, 2023. https://www.youtube.com/watch?v=gCfzeONu3Mo.

Wikipedia Contributors. 2019. "The Four Loves." Wikipedia. Accessed January 15, 2024. https://en.wikipedia.org/wiki/The_Four_Loves.

www.ingramcontent.com/pod-product-compliance
Lightning Source LLC
Chambersburg PA
CBHW010938120626
46554CB00008B/2515